PETER WALKER: EXPERIMENTS IN GESTURE, SERIALITY AND FLATNESS

LINDA L. JEWELL, EDITOR   HARVARD UNIVERSITY GRADUATE SCHOOL OF DESIGN

RIZZOLI
NEW YORK

Peter Walker: Experiments in Gesture, Seriality and Flatness is one in a series of publications produced by the Harvard University Graduate School of Design, 48 Quincy Street, Cambridge, Massachusetts 02138.

International Standard Book Number: 0-8478-1069-0

Library of Congress Catalog Card Number: 88-083840

Trade edition published in the United States of America in 1990 by Rizzoli International Publications, Inc.
300 Park Avenue South
New York, New York 10010

The Daniel Urban Kiley Fund, IBM Corporation, Maguire Thomas Partnership, and the New Albany Company supported the development of this catalogue.

Design: Jean Wilcox
Typesetter: Monotype Composition, Inc., Boston, Massachusetts
Printer: Reynolds-DeWalt, New Bedford, Massachusetts

Margaret Reeve, Curator of Exhibition Catalogues
Kerry Herman, Coordinator of Lectures and Exhibitions
Joseph Ryan, Project Editor
Susan McNally, Production Coordinator

CONTENTS

FOREWORD

Peter Walker, adjunct professor and former chairman of the Department of Landscape Architecture at the Harvard University Graduate School of Design (GSD), was the school's Daniel Urban Kiley lecturer in spring 1989. To honor the event, the GSD sponsored an exhibition and this catalogue on Walker who, as principal in three major design firms, has contributed over 30 years of built work in landscape architecture.

Walker is one of the few landscape architects who combines an active practice with an ongoing commitment to studio teaching. For 15 years, he has challenged GSD students to examine the expressive qualities of project design without abandoning human and environmental concerns. In the studio, Walker encourages students to seek sources of landscape form in contemporary art and culture, history, ecology, and themselves, rather than in the norms of contemporary practice. Through his active engagement in teaching, the ideas of students have invigorated Walker's own thinking; the process has resulted in work that is constantly evolving, fresh, innovative and timely.

With the current focus of both the design and popular media on landscape architecture, Walker's name has only recently become identified with specific projects that have received wide attention. Melanie Simo's introductory essay suggests that Walker's low profile has been consistent with his generation's unwritten code: "one simply did not call attention to oneself." Shortly after he entered the profession in 1955,

the idealism and creative formal experimentation of early modernism in landscape design gave way to a new emphasis on working collaboratively and serving the needs of the client, the community and the land. The landscape was typically treated as a background setting for buildings and the activities of everyday life. An impressive body of work resulted which was sensitive to human and environmental needs, yet seldom produced recognizable icons associated with a particular designer.

Without distinct, discernible differences in the formal vocabulary of practitioners of that era, there was little critical debate or rigorous analysis of the formal and intellectual content of specific works of landscape architecture. In the 1980s, a younger generation of landscape architects, including many of Walker's former students, began to propose radically different images and formal ideas as appropriate to landscape architecture. At last a debate—through controversy—began within the discipline. Too often, however, the commentary simply expressed outrage at the perception of the new work as abandoning environmental and social values, or merely defended the necessity of an avant-garde among landscape designers.

Because Walker's work represents both the concerns of the service-oriented era of the 1960s and 1970s, and the more recent search for new formal expression, it offers particular insights into the merits and shortcomings of both camps. Thus, the catalogue carefully examines the intentions and meanings of a few of his recent works, rather than presenting a quick descriptive overview of many of his projects. The catalogue provides an opportunity to encourage scholarly analysis and thoughtful criticism of specific works of contemporary landscape architecture.

Work on the catalogue began with an extensive interview between Walker and myself; those conversations quickly focused on the development of his intention to "objectify the landscape," to move it from the background to become a foreground event that the viewer must acknowledge and address. Walker stressed the importance of contemporary art as a source for his objective landscapes, but he also emphasized how addressing human and environmental concerns differentiated the work of a landscape architect from that of an artist.*

Four recent projects were identified as exemplary of Walker's intentions and four knowledgeable observers of landscape architecture were found to critique these specific projects. Three landscape architecture academicians—Douglas Allen, Alistair McIntosh and Elizabeth Meyer—and David Dillon, an architectural journalist, were asked not only to analyze the successes and failures of the finished works but also to describe the processes and key issues that transformed Walker's intentions into reality. Each essay is illustrated with early design proposals, when available, and images of the finished projects; quotations from the Walker interview are also inserted where appropriate. The resulting critiques offer insights into the merits and difficulties of translating Walker's intellectual and artistic intentions into inhabited landscapes. The essays also reveal how his unstated intentions to accommodate environmental and programmatic concerns can modify these primary intentions and affect the finished landscape.

In the first essay on Tanner Fountain at Harvard University, Douglas Allen examines how Walker, inspired by the work of artists such as Carl Andre, experiments with the ambiguity between object and field to mark a place within an undefined and indeterminate campus site. In doing so, Walker challenges the conventional idea of a fountain and investigates "where the line between artifice and nature, like the line between object and field, is obscured." Allen also observes that Walker departs from the objective-field pieces of environmental sculptors by giving priority, when selecting and placing stones, to creating an occupied landscape where people can sit comfortably on the stones and walk among them to the fountain's center.

Alistair McIntosh points out that the tenets of minimalist painting were used by Walker to objectify the landscape at Burnett Park in Forth Worth. He applauds the way Walker avoids the period recreation of past parks, producing instead a new set of landscape forms that embody the traditional values of refuge and contemplation, while accommodating a park's functional requirements to allow people to "sit, walk, lie down and congregate." McIntosh suggests, however, that since the minimalist techniques stress the independent status of the art object, there are limits to how the park's formal structure can address its contemporary context which is dominated by a private bank building.

Todos Santos Park in Concord, California, the most recent and the only unbuilt landscape of the four projects, is described in Elizabeth Meyer's essay as a polemic landscape that challenges the community's view of itself. Meyer demonstrates how Todos Santos, like Burnett Park, exhibits a new formal vocabulary for the public park; but unlike Burnett, Todos Santos departs from Walker's other work, relying on "irony, as well as form, for its conceptual strength." Meyer analyzes why and how the Walker and Schwartz scheme utilizes archaeological layering to reveal the discrepancies between history and present-day recall, and how the park exposes the paradox of contemporary suburban society's nostalgia for small-town life. Meyer sees the ongoing controversy over proposed artifacts for the park as "encouraging evidence that Todos Santos not only appears to the citizens, it speaks to them as well."

The largest landscape of the four, Solana—the Westlake-Southlake, Texas, corporate office park—is described by David Dillon as "an extended garden in which the landscape is as important as the buildings." He relates how Walker and the design team accommodated the values of the clients and the surrounding communities to reach a common vision of a villa or hacienda where garden, courtyard, building and agriculture contribute equally to the composition. The indigenous landscape of hills and grassland, agricultural landscapes and a historic garden vocabulary of parterres, fountains and pergolas are juxtaposed to create a "tension between artifice and nature." Dillon's essay also looks at how the sometimes differing views of the designers and client representatives came together under a common commitment to a place and a historical landscape as the important idea behind the overall design.

All four essays challenge the reader to carefully analyze not only the how but the why of contemporary landscape architecture's formal organization. It is hoped that both the critiques and a more careful understanding of the work of one of our era's great landscape architects will inspire us not only to investigate new forms and images but to understand their meanings and relationships to the twentieth century.

Linda L. Jewell
Adjunct Professor and Chairman
Department of Landscape Architecture
Harvard University Graduate School of Design

*Peter Walker's quotations from those conversations are interspersed throughout the catalogue.

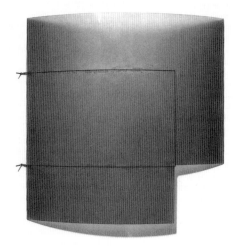

There's a world of difference between making art into landscape and making landscape into art. That's where I'm trying to be now.

1. Glass piece by Chris Wilmarth, collection of Peter Walker

Errata

This page depicts the correct orientation for the images of art shown on pages 8 and 11.

page 8
Grey Arbor for Vionnet, glass and wire, by Christopher Wilmarth, 1974,
collection of Peter Walker.

page 11
Untitled, green lacquer on galvanized iron, by Donald Judd, 1968,
collection of Peter Walker.

MAKING THE LANDSCAPE VISIBLE

Peter Walker's generation of landscape architects inherited the belief that success in the field would follow naturally from good built work. It was the built landscapes themselves that first inspired Walker as an undergraduate in the early 1950s at the University of California at Berkeley. And it was the built landscapes that his mentor and first partner, Hideo Sasaki, took to be the measure of success of a landscape architect. True, a few prolific designers had enhanced their reputations through published writings, including Garrett Eckbo of an earlier generation and Frederick Law Olmsted in the previous century. But to express himself in print did not seem important to Walker during his early career. Indeed, the post–World War II economy had helped generate such a great volume of work that there was little time for most designers to write about their own projects.

There was also a traditional, unwritten code among landscape architects: one simply did not call attention to oneself. Landscape architecture was a gentleman's profession (the field had few prominent women then, especially in the public sector). It was also a small profession, its members united by similar training in the basics—design, construction, grading, plants and history—and by commonly held beliefs in stewardship of the land and service to client and community. "Ecology" had not yet become a battle cry to divide conservationists from designers; it was rather a word beginning to be used to express environmental goals that some landscape architects had pursued, unselfconsciously and intuitively, for decades. Moreover, modernism, with its optimism for a better, brighter world, had just been assimilated into departments of landscape architecture; and earnest, quiet collaboration among design professionals remained the norm.

After three decades of practice, having survived battles over the environmental revolution, artistic expression and social issues, designers of Walker's generation have still published relatively little. "Many of us feel that until we've done something, we have nothing much to say," Walker explained. "The experience comes first, the explanation afterwards." But this modest assumption is now being challenged. Media, its users and its controllers are more powerful. In the new format of *Landscape Architecture*, as in other magazines and in the electronic media, one senses a craving for information about personalities. Landscape architects of a new generation are becoming skilled communicators, frequently publishing their work and thoughts. Walker would rather have light shed on the work and the group, not on the individual, but his colleagues have been waiting for him to speak. "I wish he'd be more communicative about his ideas," said William Johnson, Walker's former Harvard classmate and ongoing collaborator, "because I think he has a lot to say. He has always used his work seriously to explore."

Walker's current experiments, both in teaching and in practice, have evolved from

2

What Carl Andre used—and it doesn't work outdoors—were these tough industrial materials, placed on a parquet floor, a carpet or anywhere indoors. Immediately, it arrests your attention: What is that? But stick those things outdoors and they get lost. There again is the problem of landscape.

an assumption that not all of his colleagues would share: the landscape must be seen as "the thing itself," not as background. Landscape architects ought to do more than accommodate basic human needs and natural processes, Walker argues; they should strive for a landscape of meaning, a place with emotional and spiritual content. Above all, the landscape should be made visible. "Landscape is one of those mercurial things," Walker observed. "It just slips away. So you've got to bring it back, to make people attend to it. Then, once you've got the viewer's attention, you can do your magic."

Words like magic and mystery were not generally heard in Berkeley's landscape department when Walker was an undergraduate. The old Beaux-Arts system still dominated his first year, 1951–52, when his best work was a measured drawing with a few small objects floating in a large space. In retrospect, Walker sees that early work as minimal, revealing his long-felt affinity for minimum means and negative space. Ironically, the painting classes he attended were dominated by abstract expressionism, a mode in which he worked without any conviction; that kind of painting never spoke to him.

When Berkeley's landscape department adopted modernism in the early 1950s, students were taught that landscape architecture, like architecture, was to be conceived in terms of space. The students' design vocabulary was derived from the surrealist and constructivist forms found in contemporary works by Thomas Church, Lawrence Halprin and Garrett Eckbo. Landscape design history, taught without enthusiasm, was uninspiring; only modern work mattered. Pragmatism and flexibility replaced earlier ideals, since the profession was then expanding too fast for clear definitions and proven methodologies.

Although confused by the lack of criteria for making value judgments, Walker was more fortunate than some of his fellow students. Before graduating from Berkeley in 1955, he had worked part-time for Halprin and for a local nurseryman; he had designed and built a few gardens; and he had traveled with his classmate Tito Patri to southern California and then on to Mexico where he saw the austere and powerful residential landscapes of Luis Barragan. Not until graduate school, however, at the University of Illinois in 1955 did Walker gain an intellectual grasp of landscape architecture. The work and thought of Frederick Law Olmsted, Lewis Mumford, Clarence Stein and Henry Wright; Philip Lewis's interest in ecology; the buildings of Louis Sullivan, Frank Lloyd Wright, Bruce Goff and Mies van der Rohe; the great sweeping landscapes of Jens Jensen; the more structured gardens of Dan Kiley; and the cryptic, cosmic ruminations of Stanley White were all new influences that left lasting impressions on Walker.

At White's suggestion, Walker finished his graduate studies under Sasaki at Harvard University's

3

Graduate School of Design. Working at school all day and at Sasaki's office in the evenings, while raising a family, was difficult for Walker. But he was immersed in the work and loved the confrontation with modern buildings, the collaboration on new site planning projects, and the continual testing of hypotheses. According to Johnson, Walker was an outstanding teacher, even as a student. Articulate and curious, Walker would demand of his peers, "What's your *idea*?" Not all students were responsive, but Walker persisted, turning ideas inside out and playing the devil's advocate. Stuart Dawson, a senior at the University of Illinois in 1955–56, recalls similar challenges from Walker, then a teaching assistant in Dawson's class. "Pete came through like this great fresh air in the midwest desert," Dawson said. "He was a kind of moving oasis."

Looking back on his graduate years and early practice, Walker recognizes that his work was pragmatic and sometimes innovative, but not grounded in a coherent theory or strong principles. Some of his early landscape designs were not even ostensibly modern. Under Sasaki's direction, however, the procedure of

working out a design problem was orderly and highly analytical with a hierarchy of steps in the process. The excitement came from the nature of the work: rebuilding decayed city centers, and building whole communities, campuses and corporate headquarters from scratch. The older generation had won the war; now the country was ready for redevelopment by a new generation.

In some respects, what Olmsted had tried to do for America after the Civil War, Walker's generation, under the leadership of Sasaki, tried to accomplish after World War II. Like Olmsted, members of Walker's generation were more pragmatic than theoretical. Many of them struggled, as Olmsted had struggled, to reconcile aesthetic goals with social purposes and environmental constraints; and they remained more concerned about getting the job done. For Walker, as for many of his peers, the key issues of the profession were function, the setting of architecture, and the transition from the site to the landscape beyond.

A modernist to this day, Walker is still concerned about these practical issues. For the last 15 years, however, he has focused on reconciling the practical with the spiritual. He is pleased when people use his landscapes; but he is delighted when they begin to think about them, search for meaning in them, maybe even see the humor in them or the sadness. His vivid memories of some of the world's great gardens—the Alhambra, Ryoan-ji and Vaux-le-Vicomte—are of his own emotions and flights of association, not analysis. "If something gets you to dream," he observed, "it's incredible!"

Walker has now discarded one of the modernist tenets, that architecture and landscape architecture are fundamentally the same since both fields are concerned with

2. *Lead-Aluminum Plain* **by Carl Andre, 1969, the Seattle Art Museum, gift of Ann Gerber**

3. **Study for a painted wood sculpture by Donald Judd, 1963-64, collection of Peter Walker**

4

the shaping of space for human needs. "I suddenly realized that we were seeing things differently in the landscape," he said. "We have different talents, different conceptual bases, a different sense of scale, a different set of control systems." As Walker became intrigued with these differences, he became more interested in architecture and sculpture. Collaborations became more productive, sometimes even friendlier, as he sought out architects and sculptors for their particular knowledge, perceptions and skills. And Walker's own work began to change for a complex set of reasons.

Still appreciative of fine spatial design, Walker came to reject the modernist view of that universal element—space. When landscape is treated simply as space—as a suitable setting for a building or a piece of sculpture—people tend to ignore the landscape. By performing the role of servant, the landscape becomes invisible. Rather than accept this servant-master relationship between landscape architecture and another art form, Walker is now looking for dialogue.

Another modernist belief that Walker now accepts only with caution is the notion that machines are beautiful. "I remember when I first started, we read Sigfried Giedion's *Mechanization Takes Command*," he noted, "and I thought all machines were beautiful. Now I think what was meant was very much like my understanding of Mies: less *can* be more. Machines *can* be beautiful. Our problem is to figure out why they're beautiful. If they're beautiful, they reach another person's soul."

Nearly 20 years ago, after Walker had begun to collect works of minimal art that profoundly moved him, he started questioning the very basis of his professional activities. He was then chairman of the board of the SWA Group (the outgrowth of Sasaki, Walker and Associates, San Francisco) where he coordinated several design teams while working closely with one team at a time. At times he would suggest an intuitive solution; then a team member would insist on a more rational, developed process. Sometimes a job for a commercial developer would lack a certain kind of beauty—austere, serene or mysterious—which he appreciated in minimal pieces by Carl Andre, Donald Judd or Sol Lewitt. "Minimalism really spoke to me; it was so powerful," Walker explained. And he wondered how minimal art could inform landscape architecture.

In 1976 such questions led Walker to accept an offer to teach at Harvard University's Graduate School of Design, where he served as chairman of the Department of Landscape Architecture from 1978 to 1981. For studios in housing and large-scale development, he recruited other experience practitioners, including Kalvin Platt and Donald Cameron. In his own classes, Walker focused on the relationships between landscape architecture and contemporary art. His attitude toward teaching remains consistent. "You can teach as long as you're a student," he said. "When you participate with

4. **Cube by Sol Lewitt, 1974, collection of Peter Walker**

5. *Sun Tunnels* **by Nancy Holt, 1973-76, Great Basin Desert, Utah**

5

The line in landscape between objectivity and nonobjectivity is crucial. Most landscape architects don't think about it, and I think they often fail because of the modesty of their objective goals. Sometimes they fail because they don't want to be objective. They want the work to become background.

students, together with them you learn. The students always take you places you haven't been. It's fascinating."

Walker brought in colleagues such as artist Gerry Campbell, Frank Gehry and Walter Dusenbery as visiting critics. As Dusenbery, the sculptor, recalls, Walker was trying to expand the then current ideas within the landscape profession, challenging students to refine not only their techniques but also their design expression. Participating in studio juries, and later accompanying Walker on visits to Italian gardens, Dusenbery saw what Walker was striving for: "to bring the culture forward," and to bring the past forward in such a way that both past and present are renewed.

A landscape architect still imbued with his generation's sense of social purpose and spatial relationships, Walker is now working with an artist's sensitivity for particular materials, colors and textures, trying to compose a landscape that will delight the eye and engage the mind long after the program's requirements have been fulfilled. His interests in minimal art and the reductive qualities in gardens of the past have given him a richer vocabulary than that of orthodox

modern landscape design. Although an avowed modernist, he would like to see more pluralism in landscape architecture, more expression of cultural and philosophical differences. Minimalism is simply the particular road he has chosen, without expecting others to follow him. His goal is high-minded: "to see the art of our time, that which is unique to our time, expressed in the gardens of our time"; and to create gardens that participate in the art of our time. Beyond use and beauty, Walker aims for mystery, symbolism and iconic strength. He would like landscapes to be not only visible but also wonderful.

The vitality of Walker's built work is the result of many experiments, not only at the conceptual level but in the testing of ordinary materials such as wood, concrete, asphalt and gravel. It is a process of continually learning about materials, equipment, scale, costs and methods. Art school was similar, he recalls, a place where you learned about saws, glues, paints, lines and washes. "All that is mechanics," he observed, noting that mechanics have to precede poetry and polemics. "At school, I keep insisting that you're not going to get poets out of people who can't read and write. You've got to have people who are highly disciplined. They need basic design skills."

In conversation as in class, Walker's mind leaps to analogies: "I have a friend who's a dancer and he says, you learn and you learn and you learn and you learn. And when you perform, you're on automatic pilot. You know all the other stuff. All you worry about then is the music."

Melanie L. Simo
Landscape and Garden Historian and Writer

TANNER FOUNTAIN

Landscape Design: Peter Walker
Landscape Architect: The SWA Group
Location: Cambridge, Massachusetts
Client: Harvard University
Artist: Joan Brigham
Fountain Consultant: CMS Collaborative, Richard Chaix
Date: 1985

A circular field of stones, located between Memorial Hall and the north edge of Harvard Yard, stands just outside of the Science Center. A cloud of mist hovers above the circular field's interior; a rainbow is caught in continuous suspension. On the outer edge, people sit on the rocks eating lunch. Children squeal in delight as the breeze blows the mist too close for dry comfort. Asphalt paths intersect the stone field as though it did not exist. Upon closer inspection, one sees that the stones are buried, yet they seem to be on the verge of flying apart. From a distance it is an object; up close, a field formed by objects. One is drawn to its center, but cannot reach it. Wet leaves rest on the stones, the asphalt and the grass—all conditioned by the presence of water.

The seasons change. Snow mutes the shape of the asphalt and grass, yet the field remains a series of white mounds in a circle. Steam rises from the center of the field. The rocks absorb heat and the snow melts on them first, providing the promise of spring. Water turns to fire at night, as the steam and mist refract and reflect light from below.

The work itself, Tanner Fountain by Peter Walker, defies any conventional description of a fountain. In part, it is a product of the programmatic concerns of an anonymous donor who gave Harvard University the funds to construct a fountain, one that people could "interact with in a variety of ways" and would not be simply "an empty pool" during the long Cambridge winters. But its defiance of conventionality resides mostly in Walker's concern with the limits of material phenomena where the line between artifice and nature, like the line between object and field, is obscured as much as possible. By calling into question all of our conventional ideas of what a fountain is, Walker resurrects the fountain as an art form.

Before indoor plumbing privatized water and robbed it of its civic presence, the fountain was fundamental as a public celebration of the virtues of civilization itself. Subject to its own logic and bound by the laws of fluid mechanics, the fountain was nevertheless the means by which the most basic element of life was brought forth from its hidden realm and placed into service in the world. Along with the city wall and gate, the fountain was among the chief symbols of the city, serving a dual function of civil utility and sacred gift.

Technically, there is nothing mysterious about any of the foun-

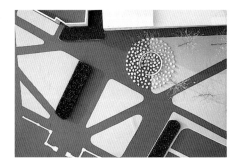

tains placed in civil service from the time of classical Athens to the beginning of our current age. Water runs downhill; under pressure, it can overcome gravity in brief but spectacular ways. Rather, the mystery of the fountain centers in its peculiar ability to tie the works of man back to a single, continuous and primary substance, and to elevate the utilitarian necessity for water to the status of a civic monument. Within the bounds of its own relatively simple logic, the fountain was free to fulfill all of its most complex and poetic duties; until sometime in the last century, fountains served as a source of tremendous artistic production.

Against this background of utility and poetic celebration, the fountain could operate ontologically, free from the constraints imposed by the weight of its own history. When water was brought indoors for everyone, the utilitarian aspect of the fountain ceased. With the demise of its presence as a civic utility, its poetic power was left adrift. Without its public and civic functions, the fountain lost its teleological capacity, and it was reduced either to civic decoration or, at best, to a symbol of its former self. From then on, no matter the complexity of the forms, nor the gymnastics of the plumbing, nor how far the limits of fluid mechanics were stretched, the fountain remained trapped architecturally between an awareness of its history and present-day water meters. With Tanner Fountain, Walker removed the fountain from this trap by liberating it from its historical limits, yet retaining all of the elements necessary for its conventional identity as a fountain.

The idea for Tanner Fountain began in 1984 when Walker, who was then with the SWA Group in Boston, was approached by Harvard University. An anonymous patron had donated funds for the construction of a fountain for the Harvard campus. Ten sites were discussed, including Harvard Square, the Massachusetts Avenue–Harvard Street intersection, and several sites off campus as well as in Harvard Yard. The site finally chosen was the unbounded crossroads just outside of the Science Center which was designed by Josep Lluis Sert. With such an indeterminate site, the problem became how to mark a boundless field with objects in a way that would make a place rather than simply another object. The ambiguous nature of this object-field relationship is fundamental to any discussion of Tanner Fountain, since Walker realized very quickly that the locus of the fountain's success would be in blurring these distinctions as much as possible. Walker answered this problem by making a figural gesture—a circle 60 feet in diameter—that was independent of everything else around it, yet participated directly with all of the disparate materials and patterns of movement found on the ground. The circle was chosen for its ability to acknowledge, through intersection, the cacophony of lawns, curbs, paths and trees already present, while remaining whole unto itself.

Walker's original idea for the fountain changed as the project

Seriality refers to the establishment of time in the landscape, like the beat in a jazz band. It is the way one establishes a rhythm around which one can organize a landscape. . . . The reasons those stones have presence is because they're organized serially. Now the serial move is not terribly obvious; the circle is obvious, but the order and size of the stones aren't very obvious.

progressed. Early on, the stones were conceived as a solid rather than a field. In this earlier manifestation, the stones formed the basin. The denial of the center did not come from the mist, but rather from the density of the stones and the presence of a wall that contained a series of jets spurting water like dandelions growing from a vertical surface. But the packed density of the stones objectified the basin more than Walker wanted, so he began pulling the stones apart, allowing the asphalt walks and grass lawns to run through the circle rather than abut it. Different geometric patterns were tried, including concentric circles, radiating rings and so forth. But the geometry got in the way of the central idea: how to allow people into the figural space, but deny them access to the water itself at the center.

Various configurations were modeled until the outlines of a random pattern emerged—clearly a circle, but one without internal geometries. The stones, each about 4-by-2-by-2 feet, were selected from a field in central Massachusetts. They were measured, drawn and eventually arranged on site in their final configuration, placed far enough apart to create a field but close enough together to retain a single objective figuration. Here, Walker departs from others who are engaged with similar issues. Unlike Carl Andre's *Stone Field Sculpture* to which it has been compared, Tanner Fountain is first and foremost an *inhabited* landscape. The stones are intended to be *used* as well as to act symbolically,

yet their use is not functionally specific: people sit on them, children play on them and students walk through them. The stones' random placement, however, prevents certain tempting possibilities: people on skateboards and bicycles cannot make their way through them. Once inside the circle, wheels give way to the human foot.[1]

The water wall at the center of the fountain went through a similar transformation, and Walker eventually eliminated it altogether. Originally, the wall formed a circle in the center of the stone field with dandelion-like bursts emerging from the wall, but the top jets kept canceling out the ephemeral spray of those at the bottom. Working with Richard Chaix in Oregon, Walker explored all kinds of spray heads, including agricultural ones, trying to get the right pressure to avoid the problem of one spray canceling out the other. Standing on a hillside overlooking the sea, Walker and Chaix experimented with different nozzles and pressures in a mock-up of the wall. Walker noticed how the setting sun was caught in the spray and how the refracted light created a rainbow that hovered about the spray. It occurred to Walker then that it would be possible to construct the bottom of a waterfall without having the top of the waterfall itself. In doing so, the stones themselves, not the wall, would be dematerialized by the water. This simple idea proved to be mechanically complex. Rather than having the water fall into a stone basin with a drain, the basin had to become essentially an

underground sump. With Chaix's help, however, the mechanical difficulties were overcome and the water wall was no longer needed.

With the basic idea now firmly in place, Walker turned his attention to the problem of the fountain's use in winter. By separating the
stones, each of them could clearly interact both with the snow and
other stones in a random but serial fashion. And the snow would melt
at different rates on different stones as they absorbed the winter sun's
heat. With the wall gone, however, all that was left of the water would
be the silent jets buried in the ground at the center of the circle. At this
juncture, Chaix put Walker in touch with Joan Brigham, an environmental sculptor and teacher of fine arts at Emerson College, whom Chaix
had worked with on other projects. At first, Walker thought that steam
would operate like the winter equivalent of the summer mist, but
experimentation proved that steam acted quite differently. Unlike water,
steam is a vapor, subject to different gravitational rules. Mist forms a
cloud that hovers, while steam drifts away. Mist is still a liquid, but steam
is a gas. Originally, the steam was to be drawn from Harvard's central
heating plant, but it proved to be very hot—too hot to pass legal muster
with those concerned about possible liability should anyone venture into
the middle of the steam cloud. Unfortunately, this issue is still unre-
solved, and the steam is not fully activated through the winter. The 32
nozzles do not generate enough density to achieve the desired effect,
but when they are turned on in winter, the effect is wondrous: huge
clouds of white vapor floating away on a cold New England evening.

By concentrating on the interaction of material phenomena,
Tanner Fountain compels us to reconsider the ancient capacity of the
fountain to act teleologically. Historical time seems to be suspended.
Instead, we are placed within real time and real space, a part of the
movement of the sun across the sky and the passing of the seasons. The
stones give the fountain weight. By burying them in the ground and
moving them apart, the field that the stones condition moves through
them. Real history is brought into the present. The stones are old; they
could have been there prior to everything else, yet we sense that they
were not. They were added, composed for our enjoyment and for this
place. This ambiguity between old and new, object and field, fountain
and nonfountain, releases the fountain from its own historicism. In its
presence, we are no longer viewers but participants. The center is suspended and we cannot occupy it. Instead, it occupies us and restores
our capacity for wonder.

Douglas C. Allen
Professor of Architecture
Georgia Institute of Technology

[1] Jory Johnson, "Presence of Stone," *Landscape Architecture*, vol. 76, no. 4, p. 64.

We finally decided that, like Stonehenge, the edge was the thing, and
we would have no internally recognizable geometries. . . . You get an
ambiguous relationship between the object and the field. We moved
the fountain to the edge and let it buzz. The fountain is made out of
insignificant objects placed in a significant way.

BURNETT PARK

Landscape Design: Peter Walker
Landscape Architect: The SWA Group
Location: Fort Worth, Texas
Client: Anne Burnett, Charles Tandy Foundation
Sculptor: Henri Matisse
Fountain Consultant: CMS Collaborative, Richard Chaix
Date: 1983

Looking down upon Burnett Park from the First Republic Bank Tower adjacent to the park's western edge, the expected view of paths cut into a rectangle of lawn is confounded. Instead, the view is one of paved walks which cast short shadows on a fragmented, sunken lawn. Shaded by drifts of trees and framed on three sides by regularly spaced street trees and granite planters, this shattered rectangle of green looks more like the surface of an abstract painting than a city park.

In summer, the grass and paths are animated by dappled shadows cast by the tree canopies. The movement of light and shade emphasizes the loose informal groupings of vegetation placed in two broad bands at the park's northern and southern edges. Orthogonal and diagonal pink granite paths form the main plane of this painterly composition. The diagonal paths do not uniformly cross the green squares. On the northern and southern edges of the park, some

squares are empty, while others are crossed by a single diagonal path, its direction alternating from one square to another. In the middle of the rectangle the diagonals run continuously across two squares in both directions, thus making three large diagonally crossed squares within the modular pink grid. After a few moments' observation, the green lawn no longer appears fragmented, it seems to lie uninterrupted below these colored lines that now float above a sea of green. On a clear day, sunlight reflects from a rectangular necklace of water-filled square pools. Positioned slightly off-center in the three diagonal crosses, the squares of water appear to flow under the intersecting lines of the paths. When the sky is clouded, the pools are empty of sunlight and the transparent water ripples the bases of the pools' tiled surfaces, the deepest spatial layer of the composition.

Burnett Park's main entrance, located off Seventh Street at its northern boundary, is marked by four sculptural reliefs, *The Backs* by Henri Matisse; the reliefs are visible from the street and placed diagonally to face a sculpture plaza designed by Isamu Noguchi. The park's main space is entered by descending a few steps into a triangular, paved forecourt adjacent to the sculptures. The view from this point confirms what was discerned from above: this is no mere drawing board abstraction, it is a masterful manipulation of formal geometry and landscape material in the service of a new landscape sensibility. A walk across the

floating granite floor requires, at first, a downward glance. Textural sub-tleties of jointed stone mark off the diagonal paths from the rest. Here, as Walker has stated, the design "makes you watch your feet in the Jap-anese sense, you have to watch what you are doing and it brings your eye down"—down to exquisitely detailed and layered landscape surfaces.

The light fixtures and benches usually seen in a park here meld into the fabric of the place. Thin water wands foam over the pools and the drifts of vegetation seem to float between ground and sky. At night, light squares located within the paving, the glowing points of light con-tained within the water wands, and the light fixtures located within the tree canopy all reiterate the visual structure of the place with ethereal planes of lights suspended in midair.

Burnett Park is a stunning display of landscape design virtuosity, but what does it mean?

Burnett Park was originally founded in 1919 by Samuel Burk Burnett who donated a city block of downtown Fort Worth for a pub-lic park. Its designer was G.E. Kessler, a landscape architect and planner responsible for, among other things, Baltimore's Roland Park, the Kansas City Park System and the Dallas City Plan. The park was a well-known landmark that provided a public forum, signaled an entryway to the downtown, and established a point of orientation where the city's two street systems meet.

In 1982, after the park had endured decades of benign neglect, Fort Worth's residents voted funds for a modest refurbishment of the park. The planned renovation was altered, however, with the design and proposed construction of the First Republic Bank Tower. With city approval to remove the street between the proposed tower and the park, the architects, Sikes Jennings Kelly, planned to undertake a com-prehensive renovation of the remainder of the original park. At that point, Anne Burnett, the granddaughter of the park's original benefactor, made it known that she wanted a new design for the park. The Anne Burnett and Charles Tandy Foundation provided the majority of the funds for the new park which Peter Walker, in association with SWA, designed and built.

Peter Walker's design for Burnett Park challenges the contempo-rary conventions of landscape architecture and serves as a starting point for an explanation of the work's physical form and meaning. Walker approaches landscape design in a consciously avant-garde manner. Working within the confines of the existing institutional infrastruc-ture of landscape design and production, he seeks to create a new landscape sensibility by transforming the artistic conventions of the medium. At Burnett Park, Walker has employed two strategies to achieve this end: combining two previously distinct landscape types— the green square and the urban plaza—and using the aesthetic tenets

Burnett is obviously an object-ground exercise—flatness is a major
issue. . . . Flatness is a metaphor for the earth. Flatness is to landscape
architecture as verticality is to building. It is a rug. In early gardens it
was the idea of the Persian carpet as a metaphor for the embellish-
ment of the land in a garden.

of minimalist painting.

Minimalism insists on the independent status of the art object. The aesthetics of minimalism assert that what a painting means is determined by what it is as a physical object—its presence as a thing of a certain size with thematically organized marks on its surface. This assertion is part of the meaning of any painting independent of style. What differentiates minimalist art is its rejection of the two metaphors that have validated Western painting since the Renaissance, *ut pictura poesis* —the painting as a text, its meaning residing in the work's narrative content, and *ut pictura, ita visio*—painting as a model of sight, its meaning residing in its descriptive content. Both modes of painting, the narrative and the descriptive, are symbol systems that use painterly codes and conventions to represent their respective contents. The main emphasis of both classes of painting, however, is on the signified not the signifier. Minimalism reverses this relationship—its meaning resides in the signifier alone. Minimalism makes visible the objective structure of painting.

Walker uses the minimalist aesthetic in landscape architecture to "objectify" the elements of a landscape. This practice strips landscape architecture of any association with previous canons of meaning and enables Walker to produce works that do not conform to accepted ways of seeing the landscape. At Burnett Park, for example, the appearance of a park lawn is made new by a process of displacement. The lawn is placed in an unexpected relationship with the paths and it is seen in a new way. In Walker's view, the lawn is seen objectively as itself. Additional new readings of landscape elements are created within the park by the same process of objectification. The layering of ground surfaces, fountains, vegetation and the planes of artificial lighting contribute to a new way of seeing the park. The objectified landscape elements become their own subject.

Walker's combination of the typical geometries used in the design of the green square and the plaza creates a new type of urban landscape, one that exhibits aspects of both of its progenitors. The formal attributes and meanings he considers particular to each of the two structures can be summarized as follows:

Green Square	Urban Plaza
soft	hard
informal	formal
uncentered	centered
"romantic"	"classical"

The combination of these two landscape types produces a form wherein the path system creates a multidirectional field and the center of the traditional urban plaza is denied. The lowering of the grass rela-

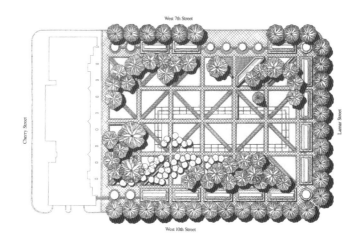

tive to the paths transforms the soft lawn of a traditional green square into a taut, fragmented plane reminiscent of a paved urban plaza. The romantically inspired placement of woody vegetation again recalls the green square, but the vegetation is superimposed onto a classical grid.

In 1985 the *Dallas Morning News* reviewed Walker's design for Burnett Park and pronounced it "stiff and cold," compared to the original. The article asserted that Walker's design no longer fulfills Burk Burnett's original intention—a "breathing place for the use of the people"—and that the original "old-fashioned city park, with benches, huge elm trees and a massive granite fountain " was a more appropriate landscape architecture vocabulary for a public gathering place. The *News* article begs the question. What makes the old design better than the new? Are parks with "curves and a few rough edges" better functionally and as a landscape representation of public space?

Kessler's original design took into account the fact that the park was surrounded by public streets on all four sides. It was heavily treed and boasted a classically inspired fountain placed in the center of the park, which served as the focus of this municipal Beaux-Arts design. Beaux-Arts design structure and symbolic decoration were used to create a natural ornament within the civic landscape. Working within an ideology (still uncritically held by many landscape architects) that equated the natural with the good, Kessler considered the visual form

of the park a representation of civic virtue.

If, in the *News* article, the reviewer suggests that the physical forms of the old park determined a type of behavior, then he forges an untenable causal link between the design form of the original Burnett Park and social values and behavior. Photographs, circa 1920, of people in parks with "curves and rough edges" suggest a mode of public behavior that could hardly be described as "letting it all hang out." Behavior in a public landscape space is not determined by physical design form; it is defined rather by social norms particular to a given culture and period. People are at liberty to behave in the new Burnett Park in any way that is acceptable within contemporary culture. The form of the park does not participate directly in their behavior.

Walker's design for the new Burnett Park is no less functional than the old; it affords places in which to sit, walk, lie down and congregate as before. No part of the park—not even the sunken lawns—can be called dysfunctional; the new design accommodates human use within its form. The landscape elements of the park, however, do not reflect an interest in the reification of use in design. The forms of Burnett Park can be used, but they are neither a representation nor a transformation of the meaning and significance of certain uses.

The new park design does fulfill the intention of its founder as a place for passive recreation. It is to Walker's credit that he has produced a park within the passive genre and has not merely resorted to the "food, balloons and benches" alternative now offered in so many public urban places. Burnett Park has not become a decorative, urban landscape setting in which the poor and rich can graze from food stands while looking for something to want. Rather, Walker's design effort has culminated in a place of refuge and contemplation within the city, but the contemplation is focused on a new interpretation of the landscape.

Walker did not design a period recreation of the old park because he does not believe that these forms can represent his modern landscape sensibility. The previous design structure of the park has been erased; no aspect of the new work manifests any overt deference to its past. This is evident in the geometry of the space and in the absence of period clutter: there are no benches, lamps or other cast-iron nostalgic signifiers of a mythic golden urban age. To Walker, a contemporary replication of these artifacts leans dangerously toward environmental pastiche. One element within the composition, however, appears to be inconsistent with his objective modern vision: the sculptures at the northern entry to the park.

The Backs by Matisse seem out of place in such a carefully designed and singular landscape. The sculptures are indeed monumental, yet one wonders if they are civic in the tradition of the placement of a statue of a local hero in a small town square, which figuratively repre-

sents a particular culture's understanding of an event in its history. Matisse intended his works for public view, but under conditions that would allow them to be contemplated as a contribution to the evolution of one of the great traditions of French art—specifically, the expressive female back. The sculptures' present location at the park's edge (admittedly mandated by the client) diminishes this meaning. They become an entry sign that signals Burnett Park, but otherwise they have little in common with the design structure or intended meaning of this landscape and nothing at all to do with Matisse's artistic intentions.

Any attempt to engage in a contextual dialogue with the surrounding urban structure is also eschewed. A tenet of Walker's design thinking is the self-sufficiency of his work which, he contends, is about the elements of the landscape and not subservient to site forces. Thus, his park design seeks to enter into a dialogue with its surroundings as a self-contained entity. The meeting of street grids adjacent to the park is not a determinant of its geometric armature, and any attempt to interpret the northeast to southwest trend of the diagonal paving as a reflection of the city grid shift is negated by the equally emphatic use within the park of a counterbalancing northwest to southeast paving alignment. The resulting figure combines with the orthogonal paving lines to produce a balanced field limited, in extent, to the boundaries of the park. It is here that the form of the park becomes problematic.

Despite Walker's contention, Burnett Park is not a self-contained aesthetic entity that relates to its surroundings as an equal. It is rather a public space that has been appropriated by a private office tower. The park was conceived as a landscape surface that denies the prominence of its center, but this landscape has a unique boundary condition: its frame is broken thereby establishing a relationship between the park and the First Republic Bank Tower—one of dominance by the tower over the park. A horizontal axis emphasized by the placement of the vegetation, the paving pattern and the fountains exists across the long dimension of the park. These elements drift in alignment across the space rather than being strictly axially organized. Yet there is an axial organization that reinforces the dominant location of the tower in relation to the park. Walker's avant-garde sensibility and design strategy have produced a design structure that is incapable of resisting its urban context. The park's formal devices have become little more than subservient foils to the building.

In Burnett Park, Walker deliberately reshaped the formal conventions of city park design, not in a capricious search for novelty, but in an effort to construct a set of design relationships that transform the way we see and value the landscape. Can a work of landscape architecture be reduced to a formal construct that is only self-referential? Can it only be involved with the objectification of its own fabric? I think not; a

The idea of lowering the lawn was to give it less weight, to make you
question whether it was a plaza.

landscape design is inescapably contextual. It must be of—and in—the world, for the discipline deals with the remaking of the world, a transforming of what the world can mean.

Landscape form and material are not separable from meaning: meaning in landscape architecture depends upon the transformation of the historical and contextual and cannot be disentangled from use. Landscape design participates in a social domain. It is a physical representation of a society's understanding of itself. A designed public landscape represents in physical form the significance that a society places on aspects of its material culture. Landscape architecture is a speculative discipline, a constant wrestle with form and meaning, but a landscape architect who deliberately seeks to transform the received formal structure of a landscape type is beholden to a simultaneous reformulation of the representation of social perceptions.

The visual form of Burnett Park has a contextual meaning that is influenced by the presence of a private building. This fact is a part of its meaning as a public landscape representation. Burnett Park is a new set of visual landscape forms that represents public leisure. Burnett Park is still a " breathing place for the use of all the people … where the poor alike with the rich may assemble as a place of recreation, particularly for relief against the heat of our summers, and as a resting spot for tired mothers with their children." The designer's stated aesthetic intentions were fulfilled, but not without unintended consequences. These consequences must be recognized.

Centered as it was about its large classical fountain, the design structure of the old Burnett Park could have resisted the presence of the adjacent building. The sensibility expressed by the previous design, however, is not the issue here. Rather, the issue is the capacity of formal relationships within their own terms to deal with contextual adjacencies.

A reproduction of the past is no longer an authentic answer for our culture. The old forms still have meaning, but they are no longer available to us in an unmediated form. The reproduction of the past—be it a classical fountain or a natural park—must undergo physical design transformations to represent the condition of modern life. Walker's design suggests that the centered urban space is not part of his avant-garde sensibility—it is unavailable to him as a modernist design strategy. In the end, the question remains: Is it not possible to conceive of a centered design structure capable of resisting overpowering contextual adjacencies that is also a work of contemporary landscape architecture, and one that, in its form, resists the privatization of public space?

Alistair T. McIntosh
Associate Professor of Landscape Architecture
Harvard University Graduate School of Design

Burnett didn't have much trouble holding. You weren't competing; it
was a void in a filled setting.

TODOS SANTOS PLAZA

Landscape Architect: The Office of Peter Walker Martha Schwartz
Location: Concord, California
Client: City of Concord
Artist: Martha Schwartz
Date: 1987–1989

In late 1987, Peter Walker and Martha Schwartz won the competition for Todos Santos Plaza, a two-acre square near the historic downtown district of Concord, California. The project has since been engulfed in controversy. This response has been surprising; what could be objectionable about providing the community's oldest public space with more grass, trees and a new playground? The answer lies in an examination of the "In the Spirit of Collaboration" competition's central question: What does it mean to propose a new civic space in a small American city?

Concord's downtown was plotted in 1867. Within its five-by-four square grid, a public park occupied a single, slightly off-center block. Traditionally, the townspeople would not only meet and converse there on market days, they would also gather to celebrate the Fourth of July and other civic events. It was the heart and identity of their community —their civic meeting ground. Surrounded by an agricultural landscape of cattle ranches, wheat fields and fruit orchards, Concord grew slowly until World War II. A prewar population of 1,300 skyrocketed, however,

to 25,000 by 1945. Today, the 108,000 residents (750,000 in surrounding Contra Costa county) associate as much or more with San Francisco and Oakland, located 35 miles away, than they do with Sacramento, the state capital. In 1970 the city christened its park Todos Santos (All Saints) "in memory of the city's Hispanic heritage," declaring it a historical landmark. Its appearance then reflected the 1954 renovations when concrete pavements and planter boxes replaced the deteriorated, wisteria-clad arbors. After the city became linked to the Bay Area Rapid Transit system in the 1970s, development rapidly increased in the blocks surrounding Todos Santos. Today, small shops front the four streets facing the plaza, rather than the major civic institutions such as a library, courthouse or church one expects to see surrounding a Spanish town square. The plaza remains significant as an open block, however, the negative of the surrounding city's built, solid blocks.

Does this formal significance—this spatial contrast—continue to reflect contemporary life-styles and to embody late twentieth-century cultural values? Is there still a need for a public gathering place in Todos Santos? In *The Human Condition*, Hanna Arendt suggests that what is public "is common [in the world] to all of us and distinguished from our privately owned place in it. . . . To live together in the world means essentially that a world of things is between those who have it in common, as a table is located between those who sit around it; the world,

I think the situational character of going in and studying a region—then making your own judgments about that information, material and opportunity—can be wonderful. That takes you away from signature, but I think signature has gotten us into a lot of trouble.

like everything in between, relates and separates men at the same time."[1] Designing a civic space, then, assumes an understanding of a culture's common ground and an embodiment of those public commonalities in a physical form. What if a people have no shared public rituals? The citizens of Concord once shared a dependence on the land and weather as well as on periodic rituals such as sowing and harvesting. Today, Concord's city planning documents describe it as a commuter suburb, subject to the "urban village" syndrome, a condition of decentralization and sprawl with no civic institutional focus. Still, Concord's citizens aspired to maintain a small-town atmosphere and hoped that the new design for Todos Santos Plaza would reflect these aspirations.

In 1985 the city adopted an urban design plan that retained the small-scaled buildings around the plaza and emphasized an Art in Public Places Program. Funded by both public and private monies, this program supports discrete artworks and streetscape elements; Todos Santos is the program's "crown jewel." The "In the Spirit of Collaboration" competition evolved within this context and directed entrants to design a "public place as art" that "retained the familiar small-town spirit of the plaza." Requested to "make art an integral characteristic of the plaza," the entrants were also given a list of programmatic needs that were determined from a questionnaire completed by 1,138 of the city's residents and workers. Those responding requested that the existing lawn and

trees be kept as the plaza's "dominant statement." The jury short-listed five San Francisco Bay area teams for the competition's second phase.[2] Although the entrants addressed Concord's history, the physical embodiment of that history varied, ranging from celebrating the region's geological history to recalling the town's agricultural beginnings to abstracting the early town plat through miniaturization.

Rather than commemorating one aspect of Concord's past or representing its history as a continuous linear process, Walker and Schwartz's winning design focused on the discrepancies between past events—history—and present recall—memory. Their design does not fit easily into the established image of public space as a green oasis or antidote to urban life, and it is not a nostalgic recreation of the civic square or village green. Rather, their vision for Todos Santos Plaza exposes the paradox of contemporary suburban society's nostalgic yearning for small-town life, despite the evidence that what is shared is not publicness but privacy and single-family detached homes, where prime-time culture and newsworthy events are delivered by the mass media, not through the public realm. What can a public place say about a community that has become a collection of individuals, unable to be gathered or separated?[3] Can a public landscape embody collective privacy and domestic culture?

Walker and Schwartz described their project as "a layering of

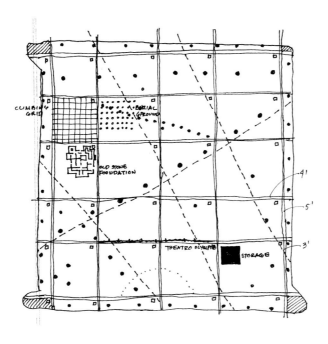

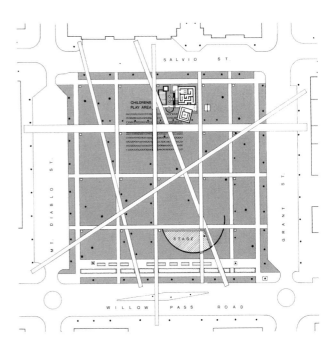

time, it functions as memory operates, where elements are not fully revealed or clearly perceived in their logical order. Our proposal is based on the idea of cumulative memory. In the same way that a fine city is a rich complex of the venerated and the new, it is our intention to build a park of layered parts. Fragments of historic images of Concord are layered to achieve a meaningful yet comforting mood of remembrance. Time is suggested by the use of various materials. These layers recall the Spanish origins, the agricultural valley period, the postwar building era and contemporary times. The park elements are composed in a constructivist collage which become the art piece."

The surface upon which this collage is assembled is a village green, domestic in scale and imagery. Orthogonal and diagonal paths cross the grassy horizontal plane just as a common's path evolved over time from necessity. These paths clearly sit atop the surface, never cutting into it. The hardened surface thus establishes the horizontal plane's significance. It is the critical object upon which the collage is assembled. The five-by-four path grid represents the city's town plat, specifically, and the region's agricultural heritage, generally.

The diagonal paths fail to suggest specific Concord references, but read alternately as a stylized network across the green and arcane constructivist motifs. Too regular and self-consciously located for a true green or common path system, the diagonal paths encourage tree

movement while maximizing the lawn areas. When movement of people across the square activates the space, it becomes a constructivist, volumetric collage equally composed of space and mass. More a place of passage than a centered, static space, the diagonal path system extends beyond the plaza's curbs into the surrounding streets and sidewalks. The paths are surfaced with eight different materials. The orthogonal paths are predominantly asphalt surfaced, but gravel, stone, brick and wood are also incorporated. The diagonal paths are made of Spanish tile, concrete block and exposed aggregate concrete. This layered history of building materials denies a literal chronology. Instead, the layers are intertwined, suggesting the layered history's artifice and the assemblage's true nature. Individual walks retain their autonomous characteristics—surface, width and direction—regardless of context. Adjacencies and coincidences result in overlap, not in combination or transformation. Like a constructivist sculpture or a minimalist work, this landscape unequivocally reveals its constituent parts.

A space implied by a tree canopy hovers atop this horizontal plane. The existing trees, London planes and deodar cedars, cluster around the plaza's perimeter; their implied lines are completed by inserting new trees. These new trees, identical in species—but obviously new, given their size—remind one of this fictive historical layering. The proposed plaza is more tree-filled and grassy than before. It contrasts with the surrounding built blocks through the substitution of vegetation for buildings, not through the opposition of space for built objects.

Under this tree-canopied space, a series of other objects are assembled. According to Walker, the unoccupied center signifies the plaza's historic role as an urban open space. Simultaneously, this noncentered space underscores Walker's self-professed "deep modernism," which continues to draw on the built works of Mies van der Rohe (i.e., Barcelona Pavilion), Louis Kahn (i.e., Salk Institute) and especially Fumihiko Maki, who spoke of modernists having the "courage not to put something at the end of an axis or in the center of a space."[4]

Around this center, which has no center, are the many program elements requested in the competition. The plaza's perimeter lawn is reinforced with turf block to prevent soil compaction during festivals when the plaza's boundaries expand onto the streets. Along Willow Pass Road, a flowering hedge maintains a civic street presence while sheltering a picnic area and a stage. Enclosed by a wooden-lattice arc 100 feet in diameter, this stage's wisteria-draped backdrop references "images of the valley's past, of the Wisteria City."

The new play structure consists of a stone-and-dry-mist fountain, and "a series of fragments representing domestic architecture." The fountain is an approximately 80-by-60 feet field of stones in which the stones appear as both objects and containers, as their carved, concave tops hold small amounts of water for children's play. A construction of fragmented, miniaturized playhouses stands next to the fountain. An adobe maze, a ruined hearth and chimney and an unfinished stud wall are juxtaposed, thus condensing the history of domestic construction. A corridor surfaced with a wooden deck and outdoor carpet connects several rooms that house slides, stairs, rope joists, sunken sand pits and bronze chairs. A stud wall and plexiglass tower, slightly rotated off the dominant grid, becomes an object within this assembled object.

The adjacency of the stones and these constructions, which represent or suggest things beyond themselves in suburban culture, imbues the stone field with a meaning beyond Walker's previous stone fountains. Associated with the idea of home, community and growth over time, the stones "form symbols of our primeval past, our primitive beginnings and perhaps a recall of people who have gone before," commented Walker and Schwartz. Edged by a wrought-iron fence, surrounded in mist and adjacent to the "home," the stones might conjure up images of graveyards, or of worlds only one's imagination can know.

Collage and viewer-interpretation form the conceptual and perceptual structure of the play area. These two conditions build on Walker's commitment to essential elements and minimal means, and on Schwartz's predilection for ambiguity, wit and found objects. More than

a visual convention, the archaeological layering describes the intellectual process required to assemble a reality from these fragments. In one's mind, what has previously been a neutral stone field is transformed through juxtaposition with culturally laden objects into social commentary and criticism. This process weds the work of Walker and Schwartz with conceptual artists such as Sol Lewitt and architects such as Peter Eisenman, whose investigations in the late 1960s and early 1970s "engaged the mind and not the eye or emotion,"[5] and in doing so, clarified the distinction between perceptual and conceptual structure.

Assembling objects to make the plaza visible is consistent with Walker's lingering modernist bias that space is ground, not figure, and as such is incapable of visibility. Seriality, the notion of performing repetitive investigations within a limited palette, is a strategy gleaned from artistic oeuvres as diverse as those of Sol Lewitt, Carl Andre, André Le Nôtre and Lawrence Halprin. Each Walker and Schwartz series exploits the landscape's perceptual and phenomenal attributes, encouraging viewer interaction and inviting comparisons with conceptual artists' intentions. Two interests not apparent in previous Walker and Schwartz projects appear in Todos Santos: the use of the archaeological metaphor and the substitution of irony for the humor that has characterized Schwartz's prior work. Both of these developments have significant consequences for the meaning, interpretation and acceptance of Todos Santos Plaza.

The Walker and Schwartz proposal relies on irony as well as form for its conceptual strength. Critics and public audiences expect works of art to contain ambiguities, ironies and paradoxes that provoke or move us. Landscapes are not expected to function similarly, at least not to the residents of Concord. To them, grass, trees and play structures should be inert objects, devoid of emotive powers and, particularly, provocation. These differences between the Concord community's expectations and the designers' intentions aggravated the usual dialogue that design commissions engender. According to one city official, the design jury chose the Walker and Schwartz proposal because their design was more like the city's old plaza than the city's old plaza itself. It responded to the request for grass and trees, and it appeared to be more traditional than those of the other semifinalists. Only later did the possible ironic meaning inherent in the few objects that were not grass and trees become evident to Concord's residents. This realization, coupled with protests of insignificant citizen participation during the competition, instigated the formation of a citizen's group, the Friends of Todos Santos, which opposed the Walker and Schwartz design.

In their October 1988 position paper, the Friends stated: "Todos Santos Plaza is a special place and one of substantial historical significance. The park was donated to the city by one of its founders more

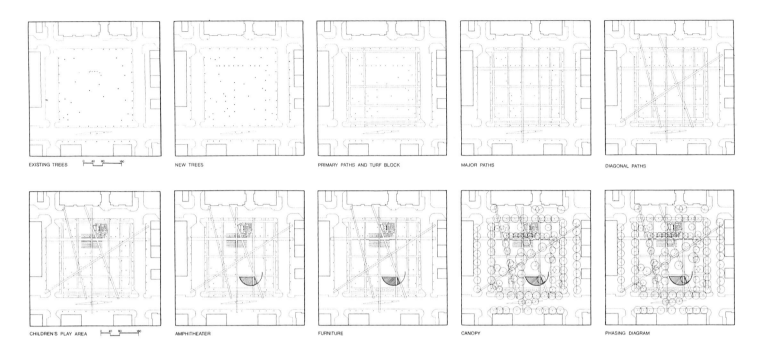

EXISTING TREES   NEW TREES   PRIMARY PATHS AND TURF BLOCK   MAJOR PATHS   DIAGONAL PATHS

CHILDREN'S PLAY AREA   AMPHITHEATER   FURNITURE   CANOPY   PHASING DIAGRAM

than one hundred years ago, long before there were La-Z-Boy recliners and plexiglass. The park is the heart of the city and we feel it should have a more conservative look." While the La-Z-Boy bronze chair struck particularly close to home, the Friends believed that the concept of cumulative memory resulted in excessive variety and unnecessary reliance on substandard materials. The heights of hedges, the wooden lattice and the play structures also gave rise to concerns about safety. Although the Friends plea that the City Council ask Walker and Schwartz to start over has not yet materialized into a directive, concessions have been made: the bronze chairs are gone, the stage's arc is smaller and there are more flowering plants along the Willow Pass Road edge. Walker is concerned, however, that subtracting even a few elements alters the concept. Given a minimal scheme with multiple functioning elements, Walker believes that these changes compromise the park or "public place as art." If the plaza is to be art as well as design, the irony of the juxtaposed fragments is integral to the artwork. Yet, the fragments that acknowledge Concord's post-World War II history disturb those in Concord who value its prewar tradition and continuity.

The Friends failed to recognize that, in the name of progress, most traces of the plaza's past have already been erased. The only history that can exist there is uncovered through a fictive archaeology. Expressed syntactically through the layering of trees, walks and frag-

ments, and semantically through the juxtaposition of images, this fiction is a fitting response to the plaza's genius loci. This strategy differs from a nostalgic small-town square recreation that freezes time and denies the present. Yet this ready inclusion of the recent past as an integral part of history is what disturbs the Friends of Concord. To them, agricultural, urban and geological history are more palatable than the history of suburbanization. They legitimize a town's history in a way that suburbanization does not.

Where did Walker and Schwartz's interest in archaeology come from? Given the similar language used by Peter Eisenman, who also taught at Harvard University Graduate School of Design from 1983–1985, one wonders if a new influence has permeated their work. In *Houses of Cards*, Eisenman states "the current work is perhaps best conceived as a series of palimpsests, a dynamic locus of figures and partially obscured traces. Site-specific and scale nonspecific, they record and respond to change .... The recent work has become involved in the generation of fiction, of histories, archaeologies, and narratives."[6]

Walker prefers to attribute his interest in archaeological layers or cumulative memory to a "natural progression and evolution of a landscape architect's inherent interest in site and context." Perhaps, but this interest has rarely been expressed verbally or formally in contemporary landscape architecture. Landscape analysis has, of course, relied on

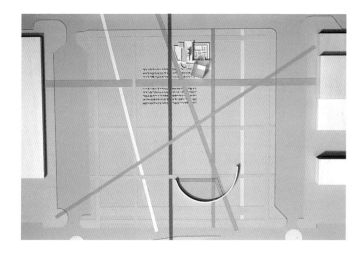

I'm very interested in the expansion of expression. You find something, you think about it. You may think of more than one good thing —*do* more than one thing—and it leads to a garden that develops.

an overlay process. But this overlay has been one of synchronic systems identically scaled and registered, rather than one of collage and juxtaposed fragments both out-of-scale and out-of-register. Those strategies, evident in the structure of Todos Santos, can be found in the Long Beach Museum competition (1986) and the Ohio State University Visual Arts Center (1983), both collaborations between Eisenman and Laurie Olin, former chairman of the GSD's Department of Landscape Architecture.

This is not to suggest that Walker and Schwartz's employment of archaeological metaphor is identical to that of Eisenman. Todos Santos diverges from Eisenman's work in ways that reflect each designer's prior works, yet each employs a fictive archaeology of layered traces, juxtaposed fragments, local historical and geographical references, and scalar ambiguities. These devices inject both Eisenman's and Walker and Schwartz's works with content found lacking in earlier formal investigations and a critical function frequently not evident in built works. Like Eisenman, Walker and Schwartz demand more of their work than formal inventiveness. At Todos Santos, the scalar ambiguities of juxtaposed domestic fragments and small-town imagery create a polemic landscape that questions the very self-concept of Concord's residents.

Walker and Schwartz's domesticated village green, a place for individual movement along multiple paths rather than a collective gathering in a dominant center, exposes Concord—the commuter suburb —for its lack of meaningful public rituals. At the same time, its grass-covered plaza perpetuates the need for small-town mythologies, at least until one scratches the hardened surface. Then, through their exaggerated down-scaling, Walker and Schwartz apply a domestic or private image to a seemingly public place. Herein lies the disturbing truth about suburbia's private emphasis. Arendt's observations are again apt: "This enlargement of the private, the enchantment, as it were, of a whole people, does not make it public, does not constitute a public realm … for while the public realm may be great, it cannot be charming precisely because it is unable to harbor the irrelevant."[7] By employing a domestic or private imagery in a public place, Walker and Schwartz have awakened Concord—and all of us—to the vacuity of the American suburban public realm. Ironically, this public void manifests itself in private associations and memories.

Walker and Schwartz have adapted a new metaphor—that of archaeological layering or cumulative memory—to explain their design process. This mental excavation into and physical interpretation of Concord's recent history departs from Walker's prior preoccupation with minimalism. Confident in his ability to overcome the modern landscape's invisibility, at Todos Santos, Walker addresses the recent landscape's inability to speak, to represent and to be meaningful. This physical montage of domestic fragments also departs from Schwartz's past reliance on

objects with specific, inherent meaning. Here the landscape's essential elements—plants, stone, land, water and mist rather than bagels, Neccos or golden frogs—are imbued with a weight that belies their individual size and being. These neutral objects make not only the present but the past visible and audible. Walker and Schwartz have discovered a middle ground between abstraction and pop culture, a state that invites —indeed, requires—the viewer to find meaning by mentally interpreting form and symbol.

The controversy surrounding the design is encouraging evidence that Todos Santos Plaza not only appears to the public, it speaks to them as well. Concord's residents, interpreting the plaza's message as pointedly ironic, may not like what they hear, but they have heard it. They may not yet have the ability to see themselves for what they are, nor the ability to laugh at themselves. Perhaps their children, who grow up playing in the plaza's ghost-like houses and misty, dematerialized stone fountain, a place seeped in memory, fantasy and irony, will inhabit a different Concord. The residents of Concord might then be changed by their encounter with this art object.

Peter Walker may be searching for objectification through visibility, but he should not discount the power of audible language, of spoken words. Todos Santos Plaza is a public place that is heard and seen—in ways not evident in previous works by Walker and Schwartz. It is a civic space that makes one think as well as feel, and it is a landscape that criticizes as well as accommodates. When these conditions coexist, landscapes can be "public places as art." And, suddenly, controversies over more grass, trees and playgrounds are not surprising.

Elizabeth Kathryn Meyer
Assistant Professor of Landscape Architecture
Harvard University Graduate School of Design

Note: Unless otherwise attributed, all quotes are from Peter Walker's and Martha Schwartz's submissions and project descriptions.

[1] Hannah Arendt, *The Human Condition* (Chicago: University of Chicago Press, 1958), p. 52.

[2] The semifinalists included EDAW San Francisco (Cheryl Barton, Michael Fotheringham and April Phillips) with Elyn Zimmerman; George Hargreaves Associates; the SWA Group (John Wong and John Loomis) with Robert Behren, Carole Aoki, T.J. McHose and David Noffsinger; and Dixi Carillo and John Roberts.

[3] Arendt, pp. 52–53. Arendt illuminates the paradox: "What makes the mass media so difficult to bear is not the number of people involved, or at least not primarily, but the fact that the world between them has lost its power to gather them, to related and to separate them."

[4] From a June 1989 conversation with Peter Walker.

[5] Peter Eisenman, "Notes on Conceptual Architecture—Towards a Definition," *Casabella* 35:359–360 (December 1971), p. 57. Eisenman quotes from the *Sol Lewitt Catalogue*, Haagsgemeente Museum, August 1970.

[6] Peter Eisenman, *Houses of Cards* (New York: Oxford University Press, 1987), p. 186.

[7] Arendt, p. 52.

SOLANA

Landscape Architect: The Office of Peter Walker Martha Schwartz
Location: Westlake and Southlake, Texas
Client: IBM Corporation and Maguire Thomas Partnership
Architects: Mitchell-Giurgola, Ricardo Legorreta Arquitectos, HKS,
Leason Pomeroy and Associates
Date: 1986–1989

Westlake and Southlake do not fit the stereotypical images of Texas. Hilly rather than flat, green instead of brown, they are dotted with thick stands of post oaks and pecan trees reminiscent of Arkansas and Missouri. For decades they were ranching and farming towns, although mainly of the casual recreational style popular with bankers and retired CEOs. The cinemascope Texas ranches are all to the south and west.

Westlake and Southlake (combined population 4,000) now provide the setting for a new corporate office park known as Solana, or "place in the sun." Perched on the northern fringe of Dallas-Fort Worth International Airport, Solana currently consists of a marketing center and regional headquarters for IBM; a village center with restaurants, shops, two office buildings and a hotel; and approximately ten sites for future high-tech tenants with a projected 20,000 employees.

Although Solana's strategic location gives it a leg up in the local corporate relocation sweepstakes, its bold plan offers fresh ideas for an intellectually undernourished brand of commercial development. Solana is not just another corporate office park, where buildings are broadcast across a site and all traces of the original place are buried underneath blacktop. Instead, the entire site has been treated as an extended garden in which the landscape is as important as the buildings, and big ideas have not been crowded out by narrow expediencies.

Solana is a joint venture of IBM and Maguire Thomas Partners of Los Angeles, who in the mid-1980s started planning the development of some 900 acres along Highway 114, midway between Dallas and Fort Worth. Initially, the partners had no specific goals other than trying not to copy Las Colinas, its sprawling competitor down the road, nor attempting to recreate Connecticut in Texas. "We knew we didn't want to mow a lot of grass," said IBM's Steven Goldmark. "We also wanted to do something regional and related to Texas."

To put buildings in a place, yet keep the sense of place, was the mandate given to the design team of Peter Walker and Martha Schwartz, Mitchell-Giurgola, Legoretta Arquitectos, and Barton Myers. The team concept came mainly from developer Robert Maguire, based on his experience with the Bunker Hill competition in Los Angeles. Although the scheme lost that competition, he was sufficiently pleased with the team approach to try it again at Solana.

The resulting team effort was an ongoing designers' summit, filled

with provocative discussions that were punctuated by the clash of egos and differing philosophies. "A tag team approach," Walker called it. "When it worked, it was very good; and when it didn't, it was terrible."

In the project's early phases, master planning fell to Myers who coordinated the ideas of others into a comprehensive plan. Ultimately, Walker and Schwartz took over the lead in planning, including most of the grading, road work and traffic studies. Maguire Thomas and IBM agreed to an overall landscape and planning budget—$15 to $20 million—and allowed Walker and Schwartz to set priorities within it.

In spite of the continual jousting among the designers, the master plan reflects a genuine consensus about goals and priorities for Solana. The overriding concern was preserving and enhancing the indigenous landscape of meadows, post oaks, creeks and ponds. These elements form the matrix—the natural armature—that will hold the project together over time.

"Southwestern ecologists told us that the huge grassland was the climax situation here, the basic landscape," explained Walker. "We were looking at the last post oaks and a degraded grassland, so we did everything to strengthen those two things to compete with the buildings."

Given this starting point, other design strategies evolved naturally. The post oaks, some of them hundreds of years old, would be kept inviolate, a natural background for all future development but a site for none. The original meadows, which had deteriorated into hard, overgrazed pastures, would be regraded and replanted in native grasses and wildflowers. In some cases the meadows would be allowed to grow up to the foundations of the buildings.

The buildings themselves could not exceed five stories and had to be tightly composed so as to nestle into the low points of the site, as though they had grown there. They would always be seen across a landscape, usually as part of an agricultural foreground, with the prairie and woods as background. The landscape was to be an object of contemplation in its own right.

Buildings and landscape would be linked by a central parkway, planted with pines, that would separate the indigenous historic landscape from the cultivated meadows and parterres of the new Solana.

The informing metaphor for the entire development is the villa or hacienda—the walled agricultural compound. This concept was articulated most forcefully by Ricardo Legoretta, who insisted on sharp distinctions between the cultivated areas and the natural landscape. Unlike the landscape of Dallas and Fort Worth, where buildings are routinely plopped into seas of anonymous space, Solana would have edges, walls and precincts. It would be Texan on the outside, but French, Mexican or Italian on the inside.

This tension between nature and artifice accounts for much of Solana's visual energy, and the drama begins where the project meets Highway 114. Instead of a conventional interchange, with stop signs and grassy medians, Legoretta and Walker created two large outdoor rooms complete with fountains, psychedelic pylons, and four sheer brown stucco walls, which resemble sections of a Richard Serra sculpture.

At 60 miles per hour, the entrance takes on a surreal quality—part Los Angeles and part Chichen Itza. The pylons act both as stelae and as emblems for the tall buildings that are not there. From this vantage point, Solana is unmistakably a special place.

Close up, the entrance breaks down into a series of smaller orthogonal spaces—rooms within rooms—filled with surprising poetic gestures: berms planted with neat rows of flowering Indian hawthorn, like grapevines in a vineyard; or fields of Texas wildflowers creeping up to the base of the National Marketing and Technical Support Center, until the building appears consumed by color. The rooms are stylized versions of fields; here agriculture becomes architecture and art.

Not everyone applauded these brash departures from traditional landscape design. The residents of Trophy Club, a sepia-toned enclave in Southlake, expressed alarm over the magenta and cadmium yellow pylons. Walker and Goldmark also had to persuade executives at IBM that a memorable gateway, even a south-of-the-border gateway, was in their own best interest.

The Texas Highway Department presented another hard sell. Although IBM and Maguire Thomas were paying for the construction and maintenance of the highway interchange, it took numerous trips to Austin to get an OK from state officials. Ultimately, they concluded that they had nothing to lose since their right-of-way was protected and they were not going to be billed for the paint.

The agricultural focus of the design was critical to winning support from Southlake and Westlake residents, who could read and understand the land far better than they could complex drawings and models served up by architects and developers from New York City.

The residents of Southlake, the larger of the two towns, were nervous about future overbuilding and the impact it would have on infrastructure and the water supply. The partners eventually helped rewrite Southlake's building and zoning codes, and even donated a fire truck to the town.

The discussions with Westlake residents took place over a fold-out coffee table in the mayor's living room and typically focused on more individual concerns. Residents wondered, Will I see the buildings from my front porch? Will the traffic mess up my farm?

What finally sold the residents of both communities on Solana

The advantage of going into a region is that you can objectively judge
what has gone on before and you can call up things that were very
early. Then you can eliminate and edit out things that have come
more recently and are not working.

were not the fail-safe regulations about massing and traffic volume. It was rather a conviction that IBM and Maguire Thomas would keep their promise to restore the Texas meadows and prairie to something approaching their original condition.

"We were committed to preserving the openness of the place," said Doug Findlay, one of Walker's key associates on the project. "We were enhancing what was there already, doing what Lady Bird Johnson recommended. We weren't starting from the mullions out."

The National Marketing and Technical Support Center, designed by Legoretta, is the clearest architectural expression of the hacienda theme. A low, rambling, flat-walled building with projecting wings, magenta sunscreens and window frames, the center makes an appropriately melodramatic statement along the highway. It is a showpiece: what CEO would not be impressed by a circular courtyard with a misting fountain, or a vaulted blue lobby that recalls Giotto's chapel at Padua?

Yet this formal complexity is also misleading. In plan, the marketing center is a comparatively simple, straightforward building: six pods arranged along a spine that is bent here and there to create visual interest. Five gardens and courtyards of varying sizes and styles separate these pods, along with a series of narrow, rectangular pools surrounded by grass and willows that evokes Luis Barragan; a gravel square with a few trees and benches on the periphery; and the walled garden with a

misting fountain, emitting primordial vapors.

The speed with which the marketing center was designed and constructed— 13 months from start to finish—provided few opportunities for gratuitous elaboration. Although the impact of the courtyards is spectacular, the effect results more from the rigorous application of a few strong ideas and a handful of basic materials: simple geometry, large trees, gravel and grass, and pools and fountains without coping.

Mitchell-Giurgola's IBM office complex is both more formal and more extroverted than the marketing center. It consists of six identical office buildings set in two parallel rows with a linear garden between, and two L-shaped parking garages that form a baroque forecourt. Giurgola broke the mass of the building into several pieces to avoid creating a megastructure, and then turned them out to the landscape to make the cloistered spaces even more precious. This basic pattern will be repeated in later phases of the IBM complex.

The regularity of the design belies its tortuous evolution. Preliminary discussions centered on ideas of cloisters, both ancient and modern, and how they could be adapted to Solana. Giurgola's model was essentially monastic, while Walker's was more collegial. Giurgola proposed a simple, green plane between the buildings that would provide a neutral setting for outdoor activity. Walker argued that in this context nature was not enough. He wanted to formalize the landscape by

The stream is the hardest thing we did. The form of the stream
came from Tony Sinkosky being there once a week, his assistant Rob
Rombold being there every single day, and going down there every
two weeks myself, drawing with a stick, and drawing again, until we
got it right.

means of parterres, fountains, hedge rows, and other elements from French and Italian gardens. Giurgola countered that this would produce a Disneyland effect, or worse, the look of a miniature golf course. If nothing else, the debate focused everyone's attention on the importance of the space and the necessity of getting it right. In the end, Walker's ideas prevailed, although the final design reveals a merging of ideas rather than the absolute triumph of one viewpoint over the other.

The linear garden remains formal, with walkways, a reflecting pool and a vine-draped pergola. A few flower pots and benches have been added, but nothing approaching the busy little village that Walker proposed initially. In retrospect, Walker is glad that he did not get his way in this space. "The most important battles are those you lose and later discover you were wrong," he said. "What I proposed—offices opening directly onto the garden and so forth—would have been too busy. Aldo [Giurgola] understood the culture of the corporation better than I did."

Outside of this central space, Walker heightened and intensified the landscape. Parterres extend a half mile from the central garden and terminate in overviews of the restored prairie. These elements are exercises in flatness that mediate between the stylized world of the cloister and the natural landscape.

Because the soil at Solana is so difficult to work—Jello in one place, granite in the next—each parterre has its own drainage system. Along the way a series of ha-has has been designed, including hedges, groves and alcoves that add mystery to the regular geometry and draw the viewer out into the landscape. Above the parterre sits a small man-made lake—a stock tank redux—feeding the creek that crawls diagonally across the parterre, as though it were part of a Miro painting.

Walker calls the creek the most southwestern feature of his design, the one element that owes nothing to French and Italian precedents. The stream snakes across the land, not in deep regular channels, but in splayed lines that reflect the hardness of the clay beneath. For all its apparent midwestern features, the north Texas landscape has a lot in common with the desert, including parching winds and five-year drought cycles. The stone that lines the banks comes from Clearlake, Texas, and it catches the eye because virtually no stone is used elsewhere at Solana. "Stone in our culture is not a building material," Walker said. "It is a high kind of decoration." And that is how stone is used at Solana, as something rare and precious, almost as the Japanese would use it. Walker and his assistants spent months selecting the stones and placing them just so. When the willows and cottonwoods grow in, the creek will become a cool retreat in the midst of the hot, arid prairie.

Implicit in this design is the realization that water in the South-

west is precious, to be used frugally, even sacredly. The same idea is conveyed by the misting fountains in the marketing center and the village center; water in this world is wispy, evanescent, as fine as sand. Many public fountains in the Southwest give precisely the opposite impression—one of abundance rather than scarcity. Solana's fountains tap deeper sources.

If the stream at the IBM complex is the most explicitly southwestern element at Solana, there are several other pieces that represent imaginative responses to other regional imperatives—the automobile and the freeway. Solana is a creation of the automobile and the airplane; without them it could not exist. By converting freeway exits and overpasses into rooms, almost sculptures, with their own independent aesthetic identities, Walker and Legoretta have suggested one way of accommodating and taming the automobile in America's far-flung corporate office parks. They have made something special out of the experience of arrival and departure, instead of leaving all such decisions to the highway engineers.

This attitude also informs the design of the parkway that connects the pieces of Solana like a spine. Walker and his engineers drove the boulevards and parkways of Texas in search of models, but they did not find one they liked. "They were all just typical big boulevards," Walker commented, "four to six lanes and ugly as hell."

At Solana, Walker chose to break the boulevard into discrete pieces, as he broke the larger landscape into precincts and then into rooms. On one side the monumental post oaks provide a kind of dense theatrical backdrop for traffic. On the other side the regraded and rolled meadows expand the edge of Giurgola's IBM complex. Over one million cubic feet of soil were moved to sculpt this part of the site, not to mention the 3,800 trees brought in to heighten it. The median is planted in pines, which create a wooded landscape and provide a screen through which drivers can view both the forest and the meadows.

The suburban landscape of the Southwest is dominated by two building types: the solitary office tower in a sea of parking lots and the solitary office tower with attached parking garage. Both are lazy market responses to the freeway and the automobile that ignore opportunities to make significant spaces even on a tabletop landscape.

Here, the developers flouted this precedent by placing 75 percent of Solana's parking in garages, thereby liberating the natural landscape for other uses. Equally important, the garages are treated architecturally, as buildings, with public faces that can be arranged to make public spaces. Goldmark said that after Solana he is not afraid to take money out of the architecture budget to make the garages into buildings.

At the IBM complex, the two L-shaped parking garages form a

The relationship between the natural landscape and the totality of
the development was a great success. I think the sympathy between
the buildings and the gardens is a good success.

monumental forecourt for the office buildings, a ceremonial plaza from which curbs, bollards, gutters and other parking lot detritus have been removed. Cars and pedestrians mingle here as they do in many European plazas.

At the village center, still under construction, Walker and Legoretta have surrounded the individual buildings with parking lots of different shapes and character, making them into moveable landscapes that control the scale of the project. One contains trees with space for cars underneath, while another is broken up with large clay planters arranged on a crisp grid. All are treated as plazas, not as leftover space, as they are in most shopping centers.

"It took a long time for Ricardo to understand that spaces were also objects, not just settings for his buildings," said Doug Findlay. "That's how we treated them at the village center."

Solana is still a fledgling development, and as such it will depend on the fidelity of IBM and Maguire Thomas to their original vision of an office park as an extended garden. All parties involved insist that they will not compromise this provocative vision by trying to pack more development onto the site than it can handle, or sacrificing design standards to turn the quick lease.

Even in its embryonic stage, Solana is more instructive than most completed projects, mainly because at its center is a commitment to place and the historical landscape as the informing elements of an overall design. These elements are not the whole story, but they are a starting point.

Equally important, the developers and designers embraced this idea at the beginning, without waffling and backsliding. They decided that Solana was not going to be a new town, or half city, half suburban development like Las Colinas. It was going to be the commercial equivalent of a gentleman's farm—a hacienda, a villa. For better or worse, they were all going out into the country to make art and to draw as much from that rural context as possible in the 1980s. Pastoral bliss is hard to sustain under the flight path of a 747 or alongside busy freeways, but the decision to be a village rather than a city lifts Solana out of the ordinary.

"I've done big landscapes before," Walker reflected, " but I've never done one where I've looked on buildings as not the most important part of the composition. I'm still interested in architecture, but less interested in it as the organizing element. At Solana, I've been able to get some of the spaces objective. The buildings are important, but you could put other buildings there and the design would still work."

David Dillon
Architecture Critic
Dallas Morning News

Highway 114

1 **Offices and Parterres**
2 **Village Center**
3 **Marketing Center**

Gesture is the idea of extension or of visual motion—anything that gestures across the landscape so that its movement can be read against the landscape.

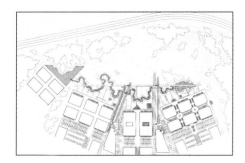

At Versailles, the little gum drops are telling you how big things are,
how vast and surreal it is. The stream does that, too. The wiggling,
natural sort of thing plays against and thereby enhances the flatness.

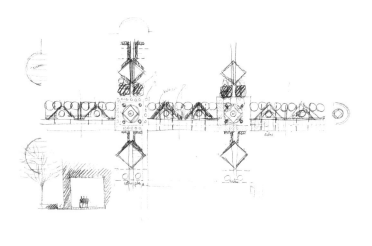

At Westlake we put benches where it was pleasant to sit, we didn't have a pattern. We'd go around and try to find places that are interesting to look at, then put a bench there. It's a perfectly reasonable way to do it; it's a minimalist idea.

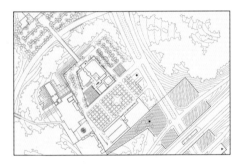

What I'm doing with seriality now is taking out as many objects as possible. There's an orchard at Solana that has a certain rhythm. Beneath the orchard we placed these concrete squares, which try to take an area containing gravel and lawn and unify it so you see both the separation of the objects and the continuity of the ground plane.

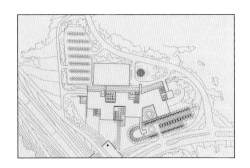

The landscape wouldn't work without the buildings, it's symbiotic. Those are the two things; it's almost seamless between the buildings and the landscape. And I think that the project so far really sits in the landscape.

I think all of us were essentially "moon men." That's a great benefit;
our objectivity was much greater. We went all over the place and
judged it. A lot of the genesis of the project was in direct relationship
to our criticism.

AFTERWORD

Given Peter Walker's prodigious energy and productive pace, it is not surprising that he has developed a number of significant new projects since we began to organize this catalogue. Several of these schematic proposals demonstrate his continuing pursuit of ideas that are evident in the four projects critiqued in this publication. Walker would be the first to point out, however, that the landscape architect, unlike the painter or sculptor, may not have the opportunity to pursue immediately the most significant lessons learned from one artistic endeavor to another. For the landscape architect, the client, program and site determine the direction of the investigation as much as the formal agenda of the designer. A look at the proposals for several new works in progress, however, clearly indicates Walker's continuing commitment to objectifying the landscape as well as to further refinement of specific formal experiments found in the designs of Tanner, Burnett, Todos Santos and Solana.

The landscape architecture scheme for the Cultural Arts Center in Fremont, California, provides a civic focus for the community. It creates a centrally located public garden that unites an existing city hall and disparately located public library with a proposed new theater and art museum complex. The buildings are an integral part of this garden landscape, but rather than allowing the buildings to dominate, the overall design allows the garden to move forward, as seen at Solana, as an object of equal formal status with the individual buildings.

At Fremont, Walker utilizes a technique of layering physical reminders of history with artifacts of present-day life. Unlike Todos Santos, the layered artifacts are neither literal nor imbued with iconographic meaning, but rather are the ordinary elements found in landscape architecture. The agricultural flower farms of an earlier era are reinterpreted as a field of alternating bands of flowering irises, meadow grasses and paths that transform the landscape between the existing buildings and the new Cultural Arts Center.

Cutting through this layered agricultural past is the new palm-lined Festival Street which is reminiscent of southern European plazas and cafe streets. The street originates in the parking lot and terminates at the base of the reshaped knoll of the existing city hall. As the street passes through the Cultural Arts Center, a dramatic wisteria and trumpet vine hedge announces entry to the new facility and helps to define the street as the central organizing space of the center's design. Here an outdoor room is formed that accommodates special performances, intermission crowds, gallery openings, art shows and other civic events. Topiary and trellises of bougainvillea provide a sunscreen and loggia at the entrances of the theater and museum, while a low garden wall separates recessed sculpture courts from the central space.

1. Garden at IBM Makuhari

An additional layer—a pathway lined with a 900-foot row of poplars—slices diagonally across the rows of flower beds as it moves toward the city's 450-acre Central Park. This linear gesture by Walker ends at a large lake and captures the park in such a way that it becomes the larger framework for the entire building and garden complex, thus transforming the park from a recreational to a civic landscape. Calling upon the gesturing of linear elements, the serial placement of planting rows to manipulate the delineation of object to field, and the techniques of historic layering, Walker's scheme consolidates visually remote public facilities into one coherent landscape. This complex now stands as an identifiable object: a civic landscape.

The Vila Olimpica is a beachfront development in Barcelona where Walker is collaborating with Bruce Graham of Skidmore Owings & Merrill and Frank Gehry to create an environment of festival and fantasy, including a luxury hotel and condominiums, a high-style shopping center, and a public restaurant and cafe district. It is part of a larger plan for a series of public and semipublic facilities that are intended to revitalize the

beaches of Barcelona's underutilized waterfront and to open up a revitalized industrial area that lies between the water and the city's cathedral square.

A major new boulevard runs along the eastern edge of the Vila Olimpica site, connecting the beaches to cathedral square. On the site's northern edge a tall steel tower designed by Bruce Graham rises to house a hotel and condominiums. A 184-foot-long, gold metallic fish designed by Frank Gehry with its nose pointing south toward the sea stands in front of the tower. Beneath the fish, a series of shops, restaurants and outdoor cafes surround a monumental pool filled with a grid of iridescent stones and hundreds of carp. Stepping back from the pool toward the hotel tower, a series of six terraces provides views out over the cafes toward the sea.

Walker designed the terraces as a series of parterres that extend the grid of the building's exposed steel structure onto the surface of the landscape, delineating that same grid on the ground in steel, stone and water and above with a series of steel trellises covered in bougainvillea. Within this grid the parterres accommodate swimming, sunbathing, dining, and nightclub facilities as well as ceremonial and reception spaces. One parterre includes a series of surreal beaches with magenta sand and beach grasses, emphasizing that the terraces are not part of a natural landscape growing from the earth but rather manipulated and artificial landscapes built on the roofs of the buildings below.

A subterranean porte cochere at the hotel lobby introduces the visitor to this above ground-below ground relationship by creating a grotto of curved steps covered with hundreds of potted ferns that slopes back to the terrace level above. The grid formed by the building and landscape above punctures this wall of ferns and is articulated

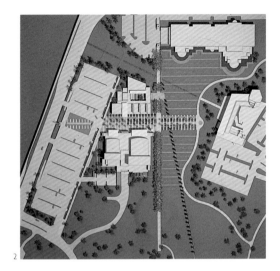

by steel trellises as well as a series of sheet fountains that spill down the grotto's back wall, bringing reflected light into the porte cochere.

Seen from the building and upper terraces, the landscape terraces become a vertical Versailles with linear parterres that appear like the mullions of a modern building laid across the terraced landscape. This articulation throughout Vila Olimpica allows the landscape to knit together the diverse architectural program elements and the distinct styles of the two architects.

El Moro, located north of Mexico City, was designed with Mexican architect Ricardo Legorreta as a modern-day Jesuit seminary dedicated to public education, research and promotion of Mexico's ecology. It is sponsored by the *Fundación Universo Veintiuno* which was founded to contribute scientific and political direction to the environmental ecology in Mexico. The foundation's first project was a set of books that examined the country's environmental issues and contributed to the support for a new set of environmental protection laws. The foundation sees the El Moro proj-

ect not only as an institution that will provide a place for ecological research but also as a place to educate and popularize the public about ecological issues.

The two-kilometer long triangular site is essentially flat and completely surrounded by a perimeter wall. Remnants of the site's former uses remain, including a farm, a nursery, an informal hacienda, a small-aircraft landing field, and a swimming and tennis club. Walker was asked not only to produce a design scheme but also a program of facilities and activities that would meet the goal of public education. Walker defines the program as similar to that for the design of a metropolitan art museum, an institution composed of people and ideas who are "one part researcher, one part educator and one part popularizer and entertainer."

Although most of El Moro's facilities are meant for outdoor use, Walker describes them as rooms of a museum that include demonstration forests, food production displays, a demonstration greenhouse, water gardens, an amphitheater for lectures and music events, a conference center, residences for scholars, and a campground. His proposal will bring in families for day visits, school children from Mexico City for class bus trips, and youth groups who will use the campground.

Walker's proposal is organized around a five-meter-high raised earthen aqueduct that spans the two-kilometer length of the site and serves as the primary pedestrian corridor off of which the series of outdoor rooms are located. The public arrives by car or bus at a large courtyard centered on a fountain at one end of the site. From here visitors pass under the aqueduct to arrive at the main entry plaza where a ramp allows access to the top of the aqueduct. They can walk the length of the aqueduct, looking

2. Festival Street originates in the parking lot, passes through the proposed new Cultural Arts Center and cuts across a field of irises and grasses, terminating at the base of the city hall knoll.

3. A pathway lined with a 900-foot row of poplars slices across rows of irises toward the existing Central Park, capturing the park and making it part of the civic complex.

Cultural Arts Center
Fremont, California
Peter Walker and Partners
Architects: BOOR/A
Developer: City of Fremont
Construction Date: 1992

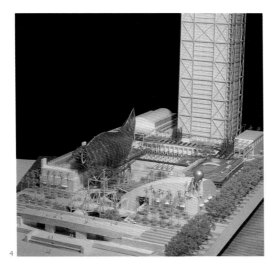

4. A series of terraced parterres steps down from the hotel to provide views south toward the ocean and to a series of outdoor cafes and shops located below the 184-foot-long metallic fish.

5. Looking south from the hotel, the tower's grid continues across the landscape in a series of water troughs that cuts through an arc of potted ferns. The troughs spill water down the back-wall of a subterranean porte cochere.

Vila Olimpica
Barcelona, Spain
Peter Walker and Partners
Architects: Frank Gehry and
Skidmore Owings & Merrill
Developer: The Travelstead Group
Construction Date: 1992

down into the activities and events on a given day, or look over the perimeter walls to the surrounding countryside. At the far end of the aqueduct, visitors reach a woods that reveals the aqueduct's water source and a small outdoor chapel.

A series of pedestrian ramps lead down into the display rooms and several tunnels cut through the aqueduct to connect the facilities on the two sides of this otherwise impenetrable wall. One side of the aqueduct structure is a sloped lawn, while the other is made of the rough-cut stone work typical of the early civilizations of the region. Walker describes the walled side as representing past cultures and traditions, while the sloped side represents a future where the enlightened use of ecological principles results in greater harmony with the earth.

Although the proposal is in an early schematic stage with the specific characteristics of many of the activity areas still to be developed, it conveys the clarity and benefits of Walker's minimalist approach. The designs for large sites too often result in proposals composed of several smaller schemes that have no

clear formal organization which makes the entire site understandable as a single entity or object. Here, the monumental gesture of the aqueduct provides a unifying point of reference as it moves across the site and defines it as an object. The facilities may grow and adjust both programmatically and formally, but the design scheme remains the same —a gigantic aqueduct placed in a memorable landscape.

The IBM facility in Makuhari, Japan, a reclaimed area of Tokyo Bay, presents Walker with the rare opportunity of designing a garden where poetic and intellectual concerns dominate instrumental issues. Both the client and the architect, Taniguchi & Associates, requested a landscape that would be a spatial work of art consistent with Japanese tradition and viewed as a contemplative object from the building. They intend that individuals might occasionally walk through the garden, but they will not linger there. The architect has oriented the important public spaces, large meeting rooms and the cafeteria to views of the 44-by-190-meter garden space that runs parallel to the front facade of the 11-story grey slate building. The building itself then becomes a screen that frames views from its openings in a manner similar to traditional byobu screens.

The client and architect did not select Walker to create a purely Japanese garden, however, but rather to introduce something of the culture of the United States, where IBM originated, to Japan. Because IBM Japan has become one of the forces reshaping Japan's culture through new technologies, it is appropriate that the garden reflects both western and eastern ideals. Walker intends to integrate these ideals by designing a garden that demonstrates, he notes, "a fusion of geometry and nature and a fusion of organic and inorganic matter."

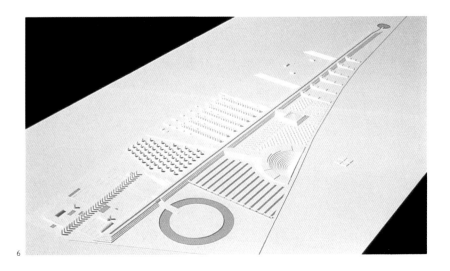

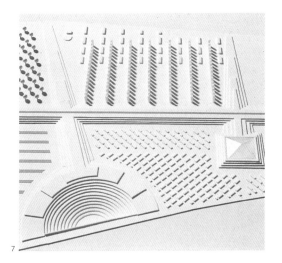

Walker also sees the garden as an opportunity to make the traditionally private event of garden contemplation into a more public and therefore more western experience. To do so, he manipulates differing views into the garden from several points of public access. He proposes that a second-story skywalk, which connects to the train station and other parts of Makuhari, becomes both a wall that defines the edges of the garden and a public belvedere with seats that provide bird's-eye views of the garden.

The garden's materials are those traditionally found in Japanese gardens, including bamboo, moss, water, stone, gravel and jade pebbles. Rather than emphasize the unique and inherent qualities of these materials, however, Walker chooses to minimize the difference between the inorganic and organic material. Here stone takes on the formal qualities of vegetation and vegetation is used as stone. The entire garden is dominated by materials in shades of green—the color of all traditional gardens. Walls of greenish slate are identical in form and proportion to the hedges that are clipped with precise architectural edges.

Traditionally, stone was used as a tie to the earth and as a symbol of permanence, but here Walker utilizes a large artificial stone which appears to hover just above the ground. Another element that indicates this is a twentieth-century garden is a constantly glowing narrow line of electric light located flush to the ground, traveling the full length of the garden and slicing through everything in its path. The light, a symbol of today's technology, has become a part of the earth while the stone, aided by twentieth-century technology, is separated from it.

Choosing to avoid the biomorphic and naturalistic forms of traditional Japanese gardens, Walker instead relies on a controlled rectilinear geometry to reflect the rational linear thinking of the West and the computer industry in particular. Grids of bamboo and long, low bands of hedges and stone walls are laid serially to clearly indicate that their placement is controlled by geometry. Relieved of the restrictions of any functional requirements—even the comfortable passage of pedestrians—Walker is free to use only visual considerations in the spacing of the bamboo, hedges and walls. His interest in the reductive nature of the Japanese garden provides the beginnings for these decisions, but his aspirations are to pursue the poetry attained in the works of Carl Andre and Donald Judd. At Makuhari, Walker embraces the opportunity to create a landscape of contemplation and mystery—a work of art that exists only for its visual and spiritual qualities.

As the reader reflects upon Walker's intellectual intentions and the visual images of his projects presented here, it becomes apparent that they are representative of a body of work which displays a continuing set of investigations relying on consistent methods and

6. Visitors arrive at a parking court centered on a circular fountain; they can traverse the triangular-shaped site atop a two-kilometer-long aqueduct from which they can view a series of outdoor rooms.

7. Ramps off of the aqueduct provide access to facilities that include an outdoor theater, experimental forests and a demonstration greenhouse.

El Moro Garden
Mexico City, Mexico
Peter Walker and Partners
Architects: Legorreta Arquitectos
Developer: *Fundación Universo Veintiuno*
Construction Date: 1990s

8. A tight grid of bamboo, clipped hedges and low slate walls frame the carefully positioned view of an artificial stone which appears to hover above the ground.

9. The garden runs parallel to an 11-story building; it has been designed to be viewed from the building, the street and the public skywalk.

IBM Makuhari
Tokyo, Japan
Peter Walker and Partners
Architects: Taniguchi & Associates
Developer: IBM Corporation and Kajima
Corporation
Construction Date: 1991

vocabulary. Walker's work is not recognized by a singular signature, but by a series of formal investigations that examine phenomena he sees as unique to the art of landscape architecture, phenomena that separate it from the other design arts.

In the manner of a painter or sculptor, Walker has developed a personal expertise through his understanding and definition of specific visual techniques. His continued refinement of flatness, seriality and gesture allow him to call upon a unique set of formal understandings when approaching each new project. The work is enhanced by self-imposed limits on his vocabulary, particularly his commitment to the reductive qualities found in minimal art, Japanese and French gardens, and the work of early modern designers. The study of specific techniques, such as the marking of an unbounded space by a series of equally spaced objects, has allowed him to understand the limitations as well as the poetic and spatial possibilities of the vocabulary he has chosen.

Walker applies these techniques to a broad range of situations, from large speculative development projects to public parks and contemplative gardens. As he tackles the unique challenges of each project's situation, he draws upon any number of previous experiments, but he allows the program, client and site to determine which techniques will be utilized and how they will be adjusted to the situation. He does not see these adjustments as compromises, but as opportunities that enrich earlier studies and lead to new variations. As opportunities and conditions arise, Walker will continue to draw upon both new variations and earlier studies to push his work to new levels of expression not yet seen in his landscape designs.

Linda L. Jewell
Adjunct Professor and Chairman
Department of Landscape Architecture
Harvard University Graduate School of Design

CHRONOLOGY

2

Selected Work, 1957 to the present

Note: Dates given indicate conceptual phases of planning and design

1

Sasaki, Walker Associates, 1957–1960

United States Embassy, Baghdad, Iraq
Architect: Josep Lluis Sert

Sea Pines Plantation
Hilton Head Island, South Carolina
Developer: Charles Fraser

IBM, Thomas J. Watson Research Center
Yorktown Heights, New York
Architect: Eero Saarinen

Upjohn Corporation World Headquarters
Kalamazoo, Michigan
Architects: Skidmore, Owings & Merrill
(Figure 1)

Quincy House, Harvard University
Cambridge, Massachusetts
Architects: Shepley, Bulfinch, Richardson
& Abbott

Foothill College, Los Altos, California
Architects: Ernest J. Kump; Masten & Hurd,
Architects Associated

**Sasaki, Walker and Associates
1960–1973**

Sidney Walton Park, Golden Gateway
Center, San Francisco, California
Developers: Perini Company and ALCOA

Carmel Valley Manor (residential
community), Carmel Valley, California
Architects: Skidmore, Owings & Merrill

ALCOA Plaza (San Francisco city park)
Golden Gateway Center
San Francisco, California
Architects: Skidmore, Owings & Merrill
(Figure 2)

Bay Area Rapid Transit District Linear Park
Contra Costa County, California; and
Albany and El Cerrito, California
(Figure 3)

Syntex Research Center and Laboratories
Master Plan and Landscape Development
Palo Alto, California
Architects: Clark, Stromquist, Potter and
Ehrlich; McCue Boone Tomsick

Seattle/Tacoma International Airport
Seattle, Washington
Architects: The Richardson Associates

Alza Corporation, Palo Alto, California
Architects: McCue Boone Tomsick

Newport Center and Fashion Island
Shopping Center
Newport Beach, California
Architects: Skidmore, Owings & Merrill;
Welton Becket; William Pereira
Engineer: T.Y. Lin
(Figure 4)

Mariner Square, Newport Beach, California
Architects: Fisher-Friedman Associates
Developer: The Irvine Company

Weyerhaeuser World Headquarters
Tacoma, Washington
Architects: Skidmore, Owings & Merrill

Weyerhaeuser Research, Development and
Engineering Facility, Tacoma, Washington
Architects: Skidmore, Owings & Merrill
(Figure 5)

Crocker Plaza, San Francisco, California
Architects: Welton Becket & Associates

Cedar-Riverside (new town in-town)
Minneapolis, Minnesota
Architects: Ralph Rapson and Associates;
Gingold-Pink Architecture, Inc.
Planners: Barton Aschman Associates
Advisor: Heki von Hertzkin

Atlantic-Richfield Plaza
Los Angeles, California
Architects: Albert C. Martin & Associates

Security Pacific National Bank
Headquarters, Los Angeles, California
Architects: Albert C. Martin & Associates

The SWA Group, 1973–1983

Buchanan Street Mall
San Francisco, California
Developer: San Francisco Redevelopment
Agency

Baywood (residential development)
Newport Beach, California
Architects: Fisher-Friedman Associates
Developer: the Irvine Company

Ethan's Glen Condominium Project
Houston, Texas
Architects: Fisher-Friedman Associates
Developer: Gerald D. Hines Interests

Promontory Point (residential
development), Newport Beach, California
Architects: Fisher-Friedman Associates
Developer: The Irvine Company
(Figure 6)

University Park (residential development)
Irvine, California
Architects: Thomas and Richardson
Developer: Stanley C. Schwartz Company

IBM West Coast Programming Center
Santa Teresa, California
Architects: McCue Boone Tomsick

Concord Performing Arts Center
Concord, California
Architects: Frank O. Gehry and Associates

Fountain at Stanford University
Stanford, California
Architects: Hellmuth, Obata & Kassabaum

Necco Garden (May Day festival garden)
Massachusetts Institute of Technology
Cambridge, Massachusetts
(Figure 7)

Roof Garden, 190 Marlborough Street
Boston, Massachusetts
With Martha Schwartz and John Wong
(Figure 8)

Columbus City Hall, Columbus, Indiana
Architects: Skidmore, Owings & Merrill

U.S. Embassy Annex, Vienna, Austria
Architects: Zimmer Gunsul Frasca
Partnership

**The Office of Peter Walker Martha
Schwartz, 1983–1989**

Cambridge Center Roof Garden
Kendall Square, Cambridge, Massachusetts
With the SWA Group
Architects: Moshe Safdie and Associates

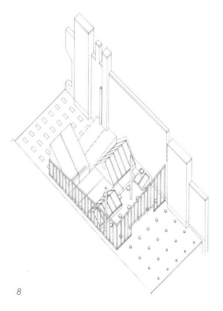

8

Vollum Institute for Advanced Biomedical
Research, Portland, Oregon
With the SWA Group
Architects: Zimmer, Gunsul, Frasca
Partnership
(Figure 9)

IBM Federal Systems Division
Clearlake, Texas
With CRSS Landscape Architects
Architects: CRS Sirrine

Regent Hotel, South Coast Plaza
Costa Mesa, California
Architects: I.M. Pei and Partners with
Gruen Associates
Developer: C.J. Segerstrom & Sons

Beckman Center, National Academy of
Sciences, Irvine, California
Architects: Skidmore, Owings & Merrill
(Figure 10)

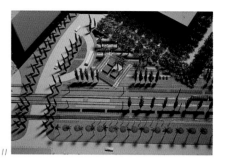

Herman Miller, Inc., Western Regional
Headquarters
Rockland, California
Architects: Frank O. Gehry and Associates;
Dreyfuss and Blackford; Stanley Tigerman

El Morro Garden, Mexico City, Mexico
Architects: Legorreta Arquitectos

Centrum Office Complex
Redwood City, California
Architects: Gensler and Associates
Developer: William Wilson Associates

**Peter Walker and Partners
1990–present**

IBM Development, Belmont Plantation
Loudoun County, Virginia
Architects: Pei Cobb Freed & Partners
Developers: IBM Corporation and Park
Tower Realty

Marina Linear Park, San Diego, California
Artists: Martha Schwartz, Andrea Blum
and Dennis Adams
Architects and Planners: Austin Hansen
Engineer: Church Engineering
(Figure 11)

Fremont Performing Arts Center
Fremont, California
Architects: BOOR/A

IBM Japan, Tokyo, Japan
Architects: Taniguchi & Associates
Developer: IBM Corporation and Kajima
Corporation

Marugame Museum and Train Station
Tokyo, Japan
Architects: Taniguchi & Associates
Developer: Nihon Toshi Sogi Kenkyusho

IBM Research Center, Austin, Texas
Architects: CRS Sirrine
Developer: IBM Corporation

Nishi Harima Technopolis, Kobe, Japan
Architects: Arata Isozaki and Associates
Developer: Hyogo Prefectural Government

Parc De Mar, Barcelona, Spain
Architects: Skidmore, Owings & Merrill
Developer: The Travelstead Group

600 Anton Boulevard Office
Costa Mesa, California
Architects: Cesar Pelli and Associates
Developer: C. J. Segerstrom & Sons

Ocean Hotel, Santa Monica, California
Architects: Moore Preble Yudell
Developer: Maguire Thomas Partnership

ASSOCIATES AND COLLABORATORS

In addition to those cited with each project, the following individuals and firms were involved in design and development.

Tanner Fountain
For the SWA Group: Duncan Alford, Ian King and Lisa Roth
Contractor: Marty Joyce, Bond Brothers, Inc.

Burnett Park
For the SWA Group: Duncan Alford, Arthur Bartenstein, Lisa Roth, Michael Sardina and Kevin Shanley

Todos Santos Plaza
For the Office of Peter Walker Martha Schwartz: Cathy Deino Blake, David Meyer, Ken Smith and David Walker
Artist: Martha Schwartz

Solana
For the Office of Peter Walker Martha Schwartz: Doug Findlay, Tony Sinkosky, Tom Leader, Robert Rombold, Lisa Roth and David Walker
Planners: Barton Myers and Associates
Engineers: Carter and Burgess, Inc.
Fountain Mechanical Consultant: Howard Fields and Associates; J. Harlan Glenn & Associates

The following individuals were former employees of The Office of Peter Walker Martha Schwartz.

Duncan Alford	Lynda Lee Lim	Martin Poirier
Terri Bahr	Alejandro Mena	Lawrence Reed
Eva Bernhard	Michael Merrick	Sandra Reed
Bradley K. Burke	David Meyer	Lisa Roth
Talitha Fabricius	Toru Mitani	Kenneth Smith
Sara Fairchild	Denise Nikas	Gina Thornton
Lisa Ganucheau	Peter Osler	Sarah Vance
Martin Kamph	Sally Pagliai	

The following individuals are employees of Peter Walker and Partners.

Partners:	Staff:	
Peter Walker	Marta Fry	Denise Rogers
Douglas Findlay	Marshall Gold	Robert Rombold
Tony Sinkosky	Jane Hansen	Kim Schumacher
Thomas Leader	Roxanne Holt	Kimberlee Stryker
Cathy Deino Blake	David Jung	Jane Williamson
David Walker	Duane Moore	Stella Wirk
	Pamela Palmer	Anna Ybarra

BIOGRAPHY

Born in Pasadena, California, on July 21, 1932, Peter Walker began his career as a draftsman and designer at Lawrence Halprin and Associates, while earning the BSLA degree, which he received in 1955, from the University of California at Berkeley. He was a graduate student and teaching assistant under Stanley White at the University of Illinois from 1955 to 1956.

Walker received the MLA degree from the Harvard University Graduate School of Design (GSD) in 1957; after graduating, he became a partner at Sasaki, Walker Associates in Watertown, Massachusetts. During 1958–59, he was an instructor at the GSD, and in 1959 he founded the San Francisco office of Sasaki, Walker and Associates.

In 1975 Walker was elected a Fellow of the American Society of Landscape Architects. In 1976 he was appointed adjunct professor in landscape architecture and urban design at the GSD, where he became acting director of the Urban Design Program for the 1977–78 academic year. Walker served as chairman of the GSD's Department of Landscape Architecture from 1978 to 1981; he continues to teach as adjunct professor of landscape architecture and urban design at the GSD.

From 1983 to 1989, Walker served as chairman of the board and principal of the Office of Peter Walker Martha Schwartz, located in San Francisco and New York City. In 1990 he founded Peter Walker and Partners, based in San Francisco.

BIBLIOGRAPHY

Recent selected publications on the work of Peter Walker and
Martha Schwartz.

Andrews, Richard. "Artists and Designers on Collaboration." *Arts Review*,
   Vol. 3, No. 1, Fall 1985, pp. 5–12.

_____. "Design Collaboration." *Landscape Architecture*, Vol. 79, No. 4,
   May 1989, pp. 58–62.

Anderton, Frances. "Avant-Gardens." *Architectural Review*, September
   1989, London, England, pp. 32–41.

Barna, Joel. "Solana's Place in the Sun." *Progressive Architecture*, April
   1989, pp. 65–74.

Boissiere, Olivier. *Herman Miller*. Unite de Fabrication et de Distribution,
   pour la region Arest, Aux Editions de Demi-Cercle, Paris, France
   1989.

Boles, Daralice. "New American Landscape, P/A Profile: Peter Walker
   and Martha Schwartz." *Progressive Architecture*, July 1989, pp. 51–65.

Dillon, David. "IBM's Colorful Place in the Sun." *Architecture*, May 1989,
   pp.100–107.

Dolden, M. "Water as an Element in Architecture." *Technology Review*,
   May–June 1988, Vol. 91, No. 4, MIT, Cambridge, MA, pp. 54–63.

Frances, Mark, and Randy Hester. "Minimalist Gardens Without Walls."
   The Meanings of Gardens. Massachusetts Institute of Technology Press,
   Cambridge, MA, 1989.

Frankel, Dextra. *Six Views, Contemporary Landscape Architecture*.
   California State University, Fullerton, CA, 1986.

Halbreich, Kathy. "The Social Dimension: Art That's More 'As' than 'On.'"
   Insights/On Sites. Partners for Livable Places, Washington, D.C., 1984,
   pp. 48–59.

Johnson, Jory. "Presence of Stone: Tanner Fountain." *Landscape
   Architecture*, Vol. 76, No. 4, July–August 1989, pp. 64–69.

Mays, Vernon. "A Park as Art in Concord." *Progressive Architecture*, April
   1988, p. 27.

Mitani, Toru. "American Landscape Architecture." *SD Magazine*, August 1988, Tokyo, Japan, pp. 6–61.

Pittas, Michael. "Contemporary California Competitions: Todos Santos Plaza." *Urban Design International*, Vol. 10, Institute for Urban Design, New York, NY, 1989.

Sasaki, Yoji. "The World of Peter Walker and Martha Schwartz." *Japan Landscape*, No. 7, 1988, pp. 92–95.

_____. "Peter Walker: Art as Landscape." *Process: Architecture*, No. 85, October 1989, Tokyo, Japan.

Walker, Peter. "Art into Landscape." *MASS*, Landscape Journal of the School of Architecture and Planning, Vol. V, Fall 1987, University of New Mexico, Albuquerque, NM, pp. 11–40.

_____. "IBM Southlake and Village Center" and "Herman Miller, Inc." *Global Architecture*, GA Document, No. 24, Tokyo, Japan, August 1989, pp. 20–41 and 66–76.

_____. "Prospect." *Landscape Architecture*, Vol. 80, No. 1, January 1990, p. 124.

"1987 ASLA Professional Awards: Tanner Fountain." *Landscape Architecture*, Vol. 77, No. 6, November–December 1987, pp. 64–65.

"1988 ALSA Professional Awards: 190 Marlborough Street Roof Garden, Westlake-Southlake." *Landscape Architecture*, Vol. 78, No. 7, November 1988, pp. 53–55, 69–71.

"1989 ASLA Professional Awards: Herman Miller, Burnett Park, IBM Clearlake, Rio Shopping Center and Turf Parterre." *Landscape Architecture*, Vol. 79, No. 9, November 1989, pp. 60–61, 64–65, 77, 91–92.